D1513777

ESP FOR KIDS
How To Develop
Your Child's
Psychic Ability

Dr. Tag Powell
and
Carol Howell Mills

Foreword by
Uri Geller

TOP OF THE MOUNTAIN PUBLISHING
Largo, Florida 34643-5117 U.S.A.

For a FREE Catalog, write, phone or fax:
Top Of The Mountain Publishing
11701 South Belcher Road, Suite 123
Largo, Florida 34643-5117 U.S.A.
SAN 287-590X
FAX (813) 536-3681
PHONE (813) 530-0110

Library of Congress Cataloging Publication Data
Powell, Tag
ESP for kids: how to develop you child's psychic ability /
Tag Powell and Carol Howell Mills.
p. cm.
Includes bibliographical references and index.
ISBN 0-914295-98-5, (quality pbk.): $12.95
1. Children—Psychic ability. 2. Child rearing.
I. Extrasensory perception for kids.
II. Mills, Carol Howell,1948–. III. Title.
BF1045.C45P68   1993
133.8'083—dc20   92-40253CIP

Manufactured in the United States of America

DEDICATION

We dedicate this book to the "psychic child" within each of us, whether the gift has been brought to the surface or still lays dormant within our loving hearts and souls. Remember that the ESP within us all is truly an untouched resource for our future.

OTHER BOOKS & AUDIOCASSETTES BY DR. TAG POWELL

Money & You (1979)
Silva Method of Mind Mastery
with Dr. Judith Powell (1983, 1985, 1987)
How to Start and Run a Psychic Group
(with Jeff Hammel) 1983
As You Thinketh with James Allen (1988)
Silva Mind Mastery For The '90s
with Dr. Judith Powell (1991)
Think Wealth... Put Your Money
Where Your Mind Is! (1991)
Slash Your Mortgage In Half (1991)
Taming The Wild Pendulum (1993)
From Poverty To Power
with James Allen (1993)
Your Daily Spiritual Guide with James Allen (1993)
Silva Master Mind Seminar 8-Audiocassette Series
Super Subliminals Plus 8-Audiocassette Series

... and over 30 other titles of
self-improvement audiocassettes

TABLE OF CONTENTS

DISCLAIMER

The techniques described in this book have been tested, and proven safe and productive by hundreds of children around the world. The methods are intended to develop, as well as to entertain and improve, the parent/child relationship.

This information is not to be used or associated with therapeutic practices or purposes, unless performed by a licensed healthcare professional. The contents and games discussed in this book should not be practiced by anyone, adult or child, with a history of mental disorders, epilepsy or fainting spells unless under direction of a licensed professional.

The authors and publisher are not liable for any misuse of this material, either intentional or unintentional.

Certain names have been changed in our case histories in order to preserve the privacy of the individuals.

FOREWORD

I was delighted when Tag asked me to write a few words as a foreword to *ESP FOR KIDS*. This type of book has been needed for a long time — to help children cope with the future ahead, to use their natural and all-too-often-ignored ESP abilities toward that future. So different are these talents from what the average adult considers possible in the world that they are often left dormant. This book, in the hands of enlightened parents, will guide their children in developing their inborn abilities, to help them get through all their difficult times.

As a child of war-torn Israel and from what is today called a "broken family," I am well aware of the many problems that modern youngsters face, and which sometimes must seem unsurmountable.

For me, even my psychic gifts were at first not gifts but an additional problem — for the spoon-bending would happen without warning! I had no control over it.

I couldn't wear a watch because the hand would move hours forward or bend and curl; sitting quietly in a restaurant would cause silverware to bend and waiters to think I was a *bad boy.*

(Looking back, I think the silverware bent because I was so psychically tuned to my mother's unhappiness when she was going through the trauma of a divorce.) For me there was no one to turn to. Like most children, I did come through these difficult times and became, I think, a stronger and more compassionate person. The God-given gifts — which in time I did learn to control — have allowed me and my entire family, as well as my two children, Michael and Katherine, to travel and experience the world and find good in all people.

Thanks to this book, the "different" child will learn that he or she is not alone in their very special "powers." From this, they will learn to develop their "gifts" and become the kind of person who can have happy fulfilling relationships with others, who can truly contribute to the world, to universal peace.

Although the world seems closer to peace than in past years, I and millions like myself know we must continue each day to pray for peace, everywhere. I desire this for my family and *all* families, and for the future families of this planet. I will continue to do my part in thought, word and deed, and encourage all whom I meet to do likewise, especially the children. For I know that our future is in their hands and their children after them.

A thousand years of peace was predicted by Nostradamus — beyond his foreboding of death and destruction. Let this 1000 years begin in the lifetime of my two children, in the lifetime of *all* our children. *ESP FOR KIDS* will help prepare our children for that future of peace. Spread the word and think peace.

Uri Geller, London

ACKNOWLEDGMENTS

We both thank God for bringing into our lives the people, events and circumstances that have been instrumental in the developing, writing and publishing of this book. Spirit has used Its Time Line, not humans, and we are grateful.

TAG THANKS

Judi, my soul supporter — giving me inspiration and the feedback needed to continue with my writing.

Yvonne Fawcett, our extremely gifted and talented creative editor. Your specific use of words can really improve a manuscript.

CAROL THANKS

Vickie, you started the ball rolling by introducing me to Reverend Lamb.

Reverend Lamb, the very first person who started my brain thinking.

Dr. Dena Gruman, your Baywinds classes gave me the help I needed and introduced me to Sally, who saw the potential and linked me with Dr. Tag & Judi.

Wanda, your search for written guidance set the premise.

Heather, you are the need which prompted me to write. You knew the answers before the questions were even in thought.

Dr. Tag Powell (and wife Judi), who have taken the basics and made it the best!

My family of Angels who helped me remember my childhood through the wonderful world of dreams.

WE BOTH THANK

All of the friends who have lent an ear. Your encouragement, ideas and thoughts have all helped in one way or another. To all the parents who sent us the case histories of their psychic children.

We especially thank the children. You are the untapped resources for our future world. You are our "psychic children" of today. May your abilities and potential grow upward and positive throughout your lives.

INTRODUCTION

We believe that the next few generations will make or break the world we know. If we are to have a future as a race and still remain on this planet, we know it is in the hands of our children. In writing this book, we hope to play a small part in shaping that future, in seeing to it that our species does continue to exist on planet Earth.

This book could be called *How To Develop Your ESP* — and we do emphasize *your* — because the training you will use to help your children may equally be adapted to yourself or any adult. The information shared in this book is based on the research and experience of both authors, as well as from international studies. We have already been asked if the book could be used as a manual for an adult psychic-training class. Yes, of course. We invite all of you to make use of this proven course of study. But for best results, do not change any technique or training method that may seem child-like — since "Fun" is a key factor we will reinforce over and over again. The "Fun Factor" is as important to the adult as it is to the child... important for success. ESP can stand for *Extra Special Play!*

ESP generally stands for Extra Sensory Perception — which seems to imply that our psychic "gifts" are separate from our "natural" gifts. We like what psychic researcher Jose Silva calls ESP... *Effective Sensory Projection.* He feels, as we do, that these ESP talents are natural... for everyone. Your child, and you, will learn to *effectively* use these normal sensory abilities — and even learn to project them over a distance, to send or access information not usually obtained, or attainable.

And do not be alarmed by the term *psychic*... as psyche, by definition, means mind. We all use our minds to a greater or lesser degree. The objective of this book is to show your children how to use their minds to that greater degree.

Dr. Tag Powell and
Carol Howell Mills

CHAPTER ONE

DREAMS: DOORWAY TO THE INNER-CONSCIOUS

*L*ewis was a young boy who experienced nightmares. His nightmares were so bad that each night he tried to stay awake for as long as possible, but eventually fell asleep, only to awaken screaming and soaking with perspiration. It was suggested by some that he was simply possessed by demons! His loving parents tried everything in their power, from warm milk to a total change of diet and even *fasting...* all to no avail.

Finally, they came to realize the only thing that seemed to help Lewis was being read to sleep. If one of his parents would read to him at bedtime and he could drift off during the story... he would remember the story in his sleep, dream about the story in his sleep.

As months moved into years this method of story reading, and sometimes story*telling*, solved the nightmare problem. As Lewis grew older he found he could successfully tell *himself* stories until he fell asleep... and then the tale would continue in his dreams.

As time progressed his *story-dreams* became more complex, more intriguing. Each morning he would write down the dreams from the night before. When he was asked to write a story as a school assignment, he would simply brush up one from his dreams. His teacher said he had a great imagination and writing talent. The fun thing for Lewis was that he could write on any subject — all he need do was start telling himself a story idea before going to sleep and then his *dream-conscious* would take over and create a fully developed narrative.

He would often start a story-idea about his friends — his "imaginary friends." These stories were the most exhilarating. Sometimes Lewis' tales were of a child's everyday life — the jobs he had to do like cleaning up his messy room or painting the fence or helping his mother. And sometimes... he even dreamed the childhood fantasy of running away to strange and exotic places. Each night, a different premise and a different dream-story.

Some mornings, Lewis wasn't too impressed with his tale, so the next night he would set up the same premise to get a *new* adventure. And like the elves who repaired the shoes of the cobbler while he slept, Lewis's *elves*... as he called his dream-makers... would construct a new tale from his old idea. His dream-adventures knew no bounds — they could range from the day-to-day life of himself and his friends to sagas of savage pirates and even epics of monsters... for now his nightmares were long behind him.

With the help of his dreams, and his daily dream-diary, Lewis went on to become one of the world's great writers. In fact, odds are you have read one or more of Lewis's dreams — *Treasure Island, Kidnapped, Dr. Jekyll and Mr. Hyde*... or the delightful *A Child's Garden of Verses*. Our Lewis was, of course, the Scotsman Robert Lewis Stevenson.

In his later years, Stevenson said he could contact "the Dream Elves" while wide awake sitting at his typewriter... by simply blurring his vision... and getting his ideas in a *day*dream. *The Dream Elves were his metaphor for his inner-conscious mind.*

This is a wonderful example of how a boy turned a serious problem into a great solution... just by tapping into inner-conscious creativity through his dreams.

> *Dreams can be one of the easiest doors to open in your child's psychic tool box.*

WHAT ARE DREAMS?

Since one-third of our lives is spent in sleep, why not teach your child to use this time to be more creative... and to even solve problems? Scientists have shown that we all dream every night, although many of us do not remember our dreams. (And *that* is what we have to work on!) Actually, the only people who are said not to dream are people with severe brain damage.

Most *dreams* take place at the ALPHA level of brain activity, when the brain is pulsing/producing a steady wave of electric current, cycling from 14 down to 7 cycles per second (cps). This Alpha level of brainwave-frequency is also, of course, associated with *meditation*, and *creative thinking...* whether produced while awake or asleep.

> Dreams are like letters, messages from the higher self to the conscious mind, giving comments on what is happening in our lives. Dreams provide a source of guidance, inspiration, prophecy, prediction and problem-solving.

You will note that your child is dreaming when their eyes, under closed lids, are darting from side to side, as if watching a movie. This is called *REM sleep*; Rapid Eye Movement takes place at the Alpha level.

Do you think you only dream in black-and-white? Actually everyone dreams in color, but too often we lose that extra punch, that special sense... because color is the first thing to slip away in morning-light.

No one knows for certain why we dream, but dream research attests to the fact that for physical and mental well-being, we need our Alpha dream-sleep. (It is not recommended that you allow the TV, radio, cassette or CD player to be left on while you or your children sleep — even "learn-ing" tapes. The sleep cycle is disrupted and can lead to irritability, memory loss, physical coordi-nation problems, and more.)

DREAM RECALL

Although many adults do not remember their dreams, this is not a problem for most youngsters. But if your older children do have trouble recall-ing, it is a simple matter to guide them to remem-ber. In their minds, there may seem no good reason to remember. Often they are just too busy coping with their "outer world." For these youths, the first step is to set up the *importance* of their dreams — by telling them how dreams can help access new ideas, develop their creativity... and help them think of new ways to solve their prob-lems! Just emphasizing the practicality of dreams will often be enough to have the older ones remember... enough to write them down and *use* them.

With your younger children, emphasize the fun and adventurous nature of dreams... as well as the wonderful ideas that will come to them, like night friends or guardian angels. Tell them about Stevenson... but leave out the monsters! And as did he, have the kids start a dream log and write in it every morning. (If too young, let them talk into a tape recorder. But young or old, don't let the "re-capping" cut into their school day.) Or have a special dream-telling session at breakfast — makes for great quality family time!

It is a simple matter for anyone, of any age, to begin to remember their dreams. Have your children, once they are in bed, say aloud:

> *"I wish to remember my dreams, and I will remember my dreams. (P.S. Please make them easy for my parents and me to understand) Thank You!"*

So be sure to remind your child to write down, talk into, or tell... as much of the dream as they can the very first thing in the morning. Dream recall/memory too often gets put aside by the problems of the day.

CREATING A DREAM BOOK

As soon as your children are old enough to write down or tape a dream, have them start their own personal *dream book*: a daily log or diary to not only record their dreams, but also their *thoughts* about the dreams. The simplest dream book can be started in a spiral-bound notebook (or for a more permanent record, buy one of the blank books found in any gift shop or bookstore). Show your child how to *date* each entry (the night they went to sleep, not the morning recall)... and *do* encourage daily use.

The practice of writing down their dreams each morning will give you (and them) some insight into their thinking. It will also help explain their problems... those which may be crying out for your attention. If you do not understand a dream, never fear, your child will be given another which will try to get the same point across.

Do be sure to invest a little time each day for discussion. These interactions truly can be "quality time" for the whole family. Although morning is best for that, if the dreams are safely written down in a log, they can be discussed later. Your child's dream book will eventually become a journal, plotting their mental and spiritual growth.

WHAT DO DREAMS MEAN?

The *unique* aspect of dreams is that the message is in *code*; they speak to us in *symbols* — the most rudimentary form of communication. You will now be learning another "language" with which to communicate with your child.

Some parents will, at this point, reach for a "dream symbol" book to try to interpret their children's dreams. *THIS IS A MISTAKE.* Everyone has his/her own personal symbols for dreams — *so* personal and specific, it's possible no one else on the planet uses the same meanings. Asking either a dream "expert" or dream book can lead in a very wrong direction.

The first dreams of the night are, according to scientists, usually a review of the day... the happenings, and the problems confronted. Next may come the mind-trips... the fantasy or entertaining dreams. These often hold a message. The last dreams before the normal awakening period will sometimes contain *prophesies*... predictions of things to come.

The mind-trip message dreams — are the *inner-conscious* trying to tell you something, trying to get the message past the guard, the *outer-conscious*. To do this the dreams are usually in code, in symbols known only to the dreamer. A mistake many people make is looking for complicated answers.

The primary way to interpret your child's dream is to realize that *since they generated it, everything in the dream is them — animate and inanimate* (when you dream, everything is you!). Your child is the writer, producer, director, actor, as well as the props, scenery and special "perspective" effects! Everything has its own significance — from your child's point of view.

Walk in your child's shoes and analyze the "action" taking place. For example, a child having a dream bicycling up a hill may mean that they are having obstacles toward "exercising" their control over where they wish to go.

If we allow them to be, the symbols are usually quite simple and obvious. So interpret the dreams with the KISS method — that's *Keep It Simple, Sweetheart.* Let the simple genius of your child hand up the answers — without the cluttering complicating sophisticated mind of the adult getting in the way. KISS!

WHAT ARE NIGHTMARES?

There is no set answer, but to look at some possible explanations, let us first throw away some of our preconceived notions.

Nightmares are not necessarily connected with negative feelings or emotions, or even too hearty a dinner! They are also not necessarily a "sign," or warning of impending danger. In the case of Robert Lewis Stevenson, it was his vastly creative imagination demanding to be unleashed. Your child (or you) could simply be ignoring this *inner-conscious creativity*, this latent talent that need be explored — and not just literary. It could be music, painting, sculpting, acting... inventing, exploring or conceiving new scientific hypotheses.

Furthermore, your child's nightmares could be the inner-conscious (formerly called the sub- or unconscious, both too negative for the true function) trying to hand up the answer to a problem of spiritual direction. Too often we are not aware of the wisdom we receive each night from our dreams... and ignore the answers which travel from the *inner-conscious awareness* to the *outer-conscious alertness* through the process of dreaming.

Think how often you have gone to sleep with a problem and awakened in the morning with the answer — which you received through a dream during the night. Yet you are often unaware that a dream helped to solve it! Your child's nightmares could have started out as a simple dream with a message... trying to reach the outer-conscious... and for whatever reason, the message was ignored. The second dream becomes more dramatic. If the answer is still ignored, the dream becomes a nightmare... with the *inner*-conscious screaming to get the attention of the *outer*-conscious. These nightmares could continue until the solution is acknowledged, accepted — and then applied (whether you consciously realized it or not)!

But let's not overlook an obvious and all-too-frequent cause of children's nightmares. Just before going to sleep, the kids have been watching television, maybe a rerun of Halloween III! The solution is for you to more carefully monitor your children's TV viewing habits. *Horror movies can cause a lot of mental, even physical damage to the psyche. It can even lead to violent outbursts in the overly reactive...*or to the child turning inward to express the terror in nightmares. A very serious result is the dying of caring and sensitivity in today's youth.

And the physical? These films (even the news!) can produce an over-load of *adrenalin*... causing more and more stress, ultimately leading to physical and emotional breakdowns.

HOW TO BANISH A CHILD'S NIGHTMARES

One of the simplest methods of banishing nightmares is to convert the *monsters* into something non-threatening. We like the technique taught by internationally known mind-trainer *Laura Silva*.

Tell your child: "If during a dream you are ever confronted, attacked, or frightened by a monster or bad person — point your index finger at that problem/person; each time

> you point your finger at the monster, it will
> shrink to half its size. Open and close your
> hand, over and over, pointing your finger
> until the monster is only a couple of inches
> high. You can then pick up the monster and
> play with it in the palm of your hand! Now
> ask the monster what he wants. That mon-
> ster will NEVER be a threat to you ever
> again."

Another solution might be to tell your children to call in *their own Dream Elves* and have
them write the monster out of the story! For older
children (and adults) all your child need do is ask
their inner-conscious to:

> "Please tell me what you want me to know
> in a pleasant dream. I'm willing to listen
> now."

HOW TO CREATE DREAM ELVES

Just before going to sleep, have your youngsters close their eyes... and relax by taking three
deep slow breaths. Next, ask them to create/imag-

ine their "Dream Elves." Allow the children complete freedom in creating the fun-loving and *protective* elves. Keep in mind to guide them away from anything threatening or monster-like... as the elves must be kept positive and fun. Have your children call them by their name – Dream Elves, such a warm and friendly name. Ask them how many there are (suggest they choose a number way under ten to keep the elves manageable).

Have your children describe each of their elves: how each is dressed and the color of their clothing, their height and weight, and what each is called. The more detail, the better your child's memory becomes... and the more useful the elves. Now tell your children to have their Dream Elves line up every night to receive their instructions... all this, while their eyes are closed... and they're drifting into Elfdom.

To encourage the next morning's dream recall, *you* instruct the Dream Elves to help the child by *their* paying close attention to the dreams... so that in the morning the elves will simply hand up the dreams to the awakening sleepy head. Don't always have it be one parent who puts the child to bed — alternate, and sometimes let it be both of you.

LET THE DREAM ELVES BE YOUR PROBLEM-SOLVERS

Dream Problem Solving is wonderfully simple, as soon as your children have repeated success in remembering and writing down their dreams. Tell them any time they have a problem — small or large (whether it's a difficult school assignment, what to buy Mom for her birthday, how to earn money to buy a new bike... or how to stop that kid down the block from beating them up!) — the children are to assign the Dream Elves the task of *solving* that problem.

And here's how: at night before going to sleep have the youngster close his or her eyes and imagine the elves all lined up, waiting for instructions. Have your child tell the elves:
"I have this problem (state the problem). I want you elves to find a good answer to this problem, and please put the answer in an

> *easy-to-understand dream I will remember.*"
> *Then off to sleep. When the youngster awak-*
> *ens in the morning, the dream-answer is to*
> *be written down in the log. Voila!*

SUMMARY

Dreams truly are the visions of the soul. Desire
to understand, help and guide your children into
becoming well-adjusted adults. Help your children get through the stages called childhood and
adolescence — become a part of their dream world,
365 nights a year!

CHAPTER TWO

CLAIRVOYANCE: SEEING THE UNSEEN

*T*he vast potential in the psychic abilities of our children are often discernible in small, seemingly meaningless occurrences or comments. Take the case of CarolAnn. As a small child, she almost always knew who was on the phone, before the phone was answered. She could tell you if it was her Grandmother Powell, her Grandmother Mills, her Daddy, or her Mom's friend, Mrs. DeBord. When asked how she knew,

CarolAnn said: "I can tell by the difference in the rings. They each sound *different.*" That's how her young mind explained it.

At Christmas-time or on birthdays, she always knew what was in her gift boxes before they were opened. She called it a "knowing" which gave her the answers. Sometimes she would dream about her gifts the night before. Her ability to concentrate on getting an answer to anything she wanted to know was remarkably strong. But this amazing strength might go unnoticed by the average parent. In fact, the parent would probably discourage such a child by pointing out the number of times she was wrong rather than praising her when she was right. And so dies the innate talents of too many children.

Little CarolAnn fits the classic pattern of a child who expresses psychic abilities. Like most of them, she was a loner — a daydreamer... who preferred the company of adults and older children to her so-called "peer group." Bored with children of the same age, CarolAnn would revert into a teaching mode, which hardly made her well-liked.

In school, CarolAnn would know the answers before the teacher asked the questions, and would tell the girl next to her. She often knew facts about historical events, facts that were not in her books — and those subjects she had never heard discussed before. The teacher disliked these actions because they were misinterpreted as being disruptive to the class.

CarolAnn began to feel she was *different*, couldn't "fit in." The children made fun of her, her teachers felt threatened by her — all of which made her retreat further within, to depend even more on her inner-self.

It is our belief that all children (every one of us!) are born with special and very precious psychic gifts. As children grow older, more "with the world," more in step with their peers... with what their parents, teachers, and the world wants of them... they lose those precious gifts. Sometimes never to get them back.

Children who are popular, accepted... are often just too busy in that belonging-state to think the special thoughts or have the special feelings. They are too busy with the here-and-now to allow contact with that special part of them — and so the talent dies.

But loner children *can* grow up to bring about major changes — in the world of art or science, even politics! So we as parents, should learn to understand, to help our children be more secure in their *difference*. That however small, their gift is the key to special beauty... to be encouraged and appreciated and enjoyed. Parents should encourage that it's *okay* for each person/child to be different... to even disagree with their peers, parents, the world. And that these *individuals* should learn to enjoy and appreciate their *own selves*... and the specialness, the differences in others. Children who are secure in this... and are free to use their gifts... will grow to become more successful adults, and offer benefit to the world.

JUST WHAT IS CLAIRVOYANCE?

There are three aspects of using our "sixth sense" and the most common ESP experience, is *prophecy, or knowing the unknowable; seeing the unseen.* In its basic form, it is our "guessing" ability with a seeming disregard for the conventional boundaries of time and space. Distance, whether in time or geographic location, is no barrier to this mind faculty.

Correct guessing, or prophecy appears to manifest in three different forms of expression, usually dependent upon the child's or the adult's strongest outer sense: sight (*visual*), sound (*auditory*) or feeling/sensing (*kinesthetic*). Just as musicians show greater talent for perhaps the piano rather than the guitar, or even a brass instrument, so too with a psychic mainly expressing their talent in either of the three aspects.

Clairvoyants are most prevalent, understandingly so, since there are more visual children and adults. Clairvoyance, of French origin, means inner seeing with your mind's eye (inwardly – dreams and visions); that is seeing clearly that which most people cannot see at all. Their visions can also be on an objective level (outwardly before them, such as auras).

Clairaudience means the hearing of voices or messages in one's inner ear without the person speaking aloud (Joan of Arc heard the voice of God). The message can be inwardly heard with or without the message sender being present – there are no time or space barriers to Mind. Some parents have testified that they heard "in their heads" their children's cry for help before they were notified of their having been hurt in accidents.

Clairsensience means to have the emotional feeling, or inner knowing (which can manifest sensations in the physical body) of events which are unknowable (through dowsing instruments, rods and pendulums). Individuals who are empathic to people and events are called "sensitives." Extreme sensitives, may feel emotional highs and lows, swaying with their environment of people, places and things, as well as exhilarating physical sensations of chills, hot flashes, foreboding feelings and highs and lows of physical energy levels. Some Clairsensients can even smell odors/scents not present in the "physical world."

Precognition is the term most used to encompass these three categories of obtaining information before the actual occurrence of the event; to know ahead of time.

Children, as a rule, score better on ESP tests, such as the classic ESP deck of cards (using symbols) developed by J. B. Rhine. Perhaps because they are not limited by notions that ESP is an unusual or even a nonexistent ability. More specifically, smaller children accept ESP and their ability to make accurate guesses without inhibition. Whereas adolescents and adults are apt to be ESP self-conscious while they are guessing. Inspire your children with the challenges of the ESP games with some type of reward or bonus. Challenges and rewards are often related to high accuracy.

Now let's examine simple and fun ways to help your children hold onto and enhance those psychic gifts.

"WHO'S ON THE TELEPHONE" GAME

Before anyone answers the phone, ask your children to "guess" who's calling.

Rules of the game:

A. Tell the young ones the "answer" must be the first thing that pops into their heads. And that they have to say the name before you pick up the phone. This teaches them to think fast and to trust their first answers... their intuitive minds. Research has shown that if a child (or adult!) takes time to use logic — such as, it's ten o'clock and grandmother always calls at ten or it's five o'clock and daddy just got off work — these "logical" left brain answers will cut down accuracy in using the inner mind (the *right* brain, the creative intuitive side).

> *Remember:*
> *The First Thought That Comes To Mind.*

B. Make the Phone Game one in which they can win — *reinforce* the "correct psychic-hits." Even if they are wrong, look for something correct: "You said Daddy and it is a man calling from the store and Daddy is a man. You are right; it is a man, very good." *NEVER tell the child that he or she is wrong; simply say "you will do even better next time."*

C. When they are totally right, be very enthusiastic; make a big thing out of it. *Reinforce the child's intuition with your positive response.* When the phone rings again, say "you were right last time; who is it this time?"

"WHAT'S IN THE GIFT BOX" *GAME*

At any time when your child (or someone else in the room) receives a gift, ask the child to *guess* what's in the box. Be sure to ask: "What color is it? What is it made of? Is it handmade or machine-made?" Always encourage the child to *say the first thing that comes to mind.* Don't let the child feel the weight of the box or shake it... as this gives too much logical data and will hinder the development of your young budding *psychic.*

The same positive rules apply here as in the "Whose on the Phone" game. If their guesses are off, try to find some point of similarity: "It does have some red... you were right, it's a soft item." Look for points of agreement and success — not disagreement and failure. And when they do score a direct *hit,* be jubilant! Praise that success.

"GUESS THE END OF THE MOVIE" GAME

This one is a fun game for any age. Everyone sits around the television set and guesses "who done it"... "or which dashing fellow will the heroine marry"... or "will he discover the secret of the ancient tomb before the 'natives' cook him? Et cetera, et cetera! At the end of the month, the one with the most "hits" gets a prize — a free trip to the theater, with popcorn!

The rule is: Everyone has to write down his or her guess beforehand... so there can't be any "Oh, I was going to say that!"

And be sure you don't play this game in the movie theater — unless you write the answers in the dark, QUIETLY.

OTHER GAMES TO TEST & DEVELOP YOUR CHILD'S ESP

"IT'S IN THE CARDS" GAME

Dr. Rhine spent his life conducting research in the 1930's that fully explored the existence of non-physical or psychic communications. He called it *Extrasensory Perception*. He used objective tests that could be statistically measured. We are not bound by the requirements of statistical measurement to prove our children's psychic abilities.

If you wish to make card tests, it isn't necessary to use an ESP deck. A plain deck of playing cards will do the job admirably. The first series to run is to have your child guess the color of the cards — red or black. They have a 50-50 chance of correct "hits." Look for results that are significantly different. Next, aim for the four suits — clubs, spades, hearts and diamonds. After that, if you are wanting to aim for greater complexity, your child can guess the exact numbers or pictures on the cards as well.

We suggest that you keep card tests short and very limited, as they tend to get boring. The mind can work up enthusiasm for a short time, and then boredom sets in. When that happens, the percentage of correct guesses decreases, results begin to get progressively worse.

"BROWN BAGGIN' FOR FUN"

An enjoyable game with our children involves an ordinary paper bag and some object (Tag's wife, Judi, used to play this with the neighborhood kids when she was a child). Prepare a paper bag that will stand alone. Inside of it, place an object — a marble, olive, pen, block or ring, etc. Your child then places their hands on either side of the bag, without physically touching it. The idea is to have them tell you what kind of vibrations they are feeling. The more they play this game, the better they will get at it.

A good variation of this game is to place various precious and semi-precious stones and metals inside of the bag. Your child will get the "feel" of these minerals and expand their knowledge with *mental* points of reference.

"GUESS THE COLOR OF THE MARBLE" GAME

Along similar lines is a game which involves "eyeless sight." Fill a bag with colored marbles of the same size. Have your child reach in and pull out a marble and guess the color BEFORE they open their hand to show the marble.

The next game is to put marbles of all the SAME color into a bag then put in one marble of a different color — in the beginning, make it a color of the opposite spectrum (all blue marbles with one red marble). Then have your child reach in and feel for the different, odd-colored marble. This game helps develop *sensitivity to color vibrations.*

ON WITH THE GAMES. The next phase is to take the grab-bag with several colors of marbles, and have your child decide beforehand what colors they are going to draw out of the bag. You may want to have them pick out three marbles and keep them in the closed palm of their hand. In that case, ask them if they think they got the marble that they were aiming for. They may tell you that they did not get what they were intending to draw. Then ask them to guess what color they did draw.

"GET IN TOUCH" GAME

Another "eyeless sight" experiment that is easy to perform involves pictures. Full page pictures or advertisements from magazines will be needed. The pictures should have only one central image. The pictures should be kept out of sight until your child is relaxed, with eyes closed (blind-folded if they tend to "peek"). Place your child's hands and fingers around the picture, ask your child what impressions they are receiving.

Have them guess what or who is in the photo-graph. Continue with photos.

SUMMARY

Learning can be fun! As you help your child increase their intuitive ability through playing games — when they are not under any pressure — then this "guessing" ability will be primed when it is most important. *Test taking, decision-making, finding life's directions, and even finding lost items — all these and more are made easier for your children when they are in touch with their inner-self.*

You can all have fun looking for new variations on the simple games in this chapter. For example: if you've lost your direction while driv-ing, ask your child if you should go right... or left... or straight ahead. Question-and-Answer board games are excellent to help your children (and you) develop more of their inner talents of telepathy and prophesy.

The more time you take with your youngster for these games, the better communication you establish... you create a physical- and mind-link. This special attention from you will help your young ones grow into a more secure and confi-dent adult.

CHAPTER THREE

MEDITATION FOR KIDS

*B*e still and listen... It has been said the difference between prayer and meditation is that *prayer is talking to God* and *meditation is listening to God*. Most of us at one time or another talk to God... but how often do we listen?

So often we are told "It's time to have a moment of silent prayer," but how often do we hear anyone suggest a moment for silent meditation? It's almost as if many religious leaders in the West don't want us to *listen* or *think* without the personal guidance of an intermediary. Are the spiritual leaders the only ones who can listen for instruction? How did the ministers and priests get their guidance *without* listening? And what if they heard wrong, or misinterpreted the message?

Earthly or heavenly, conversing or praying... the major problem is too much talking and not enough listening. If there was only one gift we could bestow on our children, it should be *the talent of listening*. Listening on both the Inner and Outer conscious levels. Parents can bestow this listening gift by teaching the child to *meditate*, the daily practice of which will give greater self-assurance... self-and-other awareness... more by way of contact with one's power of creativity... and yes, an increased spiritual development.

The problem part about "listening" on any level today is that *sound* is bombarding us, especially our kids. They seem to live in surround-sound. Music so constant, so loud it threatens to cause damage to ear drums. Music while studying, while riding, while skating, while walking, even in school! Their ears are being blasted and we parents don't even know it to warn them all — because of earphones attached to tape decks, radios, TV. This music has proven to be not only the cause of increased deafness in our young but also ear infections leading to deafness! The expression "You can't hear yourself think" has new meaning for this generation.

More frightening yet for our American youth, once the brightest and most creative, is the shocking rate at which they are falling behind many Third World nations (out of 150 nations, we rank 49th in reading!). We are graduating high school students who cannot read or write; many drop out even *before* high school. Our colleges have had to lower their standards to compensate for the lower educational level of applying students. It's not just our youth — creativity and inventiveness in the United States generally has fallen to an all-time low. *The Wall Street Journal* reported that the Ford Motor Company in the past year received the lowest number of suggestions to improve the automobile than they have received in thirty years! The alarm bell is ringing throughout our country for this growing epidemic of "creativity block." We must do something ... now. We must stop the downward spiral of our intellectual existence... before we end up on the dump heap of western civilization!

There are solutions. One that more and more people, even families, are turning to is *meditation*. *(The family that meditates together stays together; it's been tested and proven!)* Research has shown that during the meditative state not only is there a great increase in the creative process but learning itself becomes easier, less stressful. *Life becomes less stressful.*

JUST WHAT IS MEDITATION?

Meditation is different things to different people. To some folks it's a way of momentarily escaping the confusion, the tension and stress of this world. To others it's a religious discipline. Still others find it a way to focus and develop a higher thought pattern for problem-solving and increased creativity.

Almost every genius has used some form of meditation. One of the most delightful stories is about Archimedes, the famous third century B.C. Greek mathematician and inventor. It is told that while daydreaming in his bath, the concept for the *displacement of water* just "came" to him — he leaped up, shouting Eureka! which in Greek means, "I've found it!"

Leonardo Da Vinci, famous not only for his paintings of *The Last Supper* and the *Mona Lisa*, but also for his astounding designs — which include the tank, the helicopter and the contact lens! He had said that his ideas "came" to him while Laying on his back in a semi-dark room with a candle burning on each side of him.

Thomas Edison was famous for his *catnaps*, but few knew the true secret of his ideas. In a letter Edison sent to the Smithsonian Museum, he wrote that his ideas "came" to him from the *twilight state* between full consciousness and sleep. When wrestling with an invention problem, he would sit in a comfortable chair or on his day bed, with a ball-bearing in his hand and a tin pie plate on the floor. He would relax, with his arm extended over the pie plate. Eventually, as he approached the deeper level, sleep, his hand would open and the released ball would fall into the tin plate... with a crash. He would open his eyes, pick up the ball and repeat the process if the answer still eluded him... or go back to work on his invention with the problem solved. Edison was using the ball-bearing as a device to remain conscious and in the meditative state in order not to drift off to sleep.

We know his method worked because of the thousands of patents recorded in his name.

Albert Einstein reported that his ideas "came" to him when he would relax... sitting on his front porch at night... staring at the stars. It was meditating on a star that gave this genius answers to the universe.

Theodore H. Maiman in the 1960's built the first laser, the ruby laser — which has led to such modern spectaculars as light shows and microscopic surgery! He reported that the idea "came" to him while relaxing on a park bench gazing off into space.

These are only a few of the great minds reporting that quiet thinking time was the secret of their success.

In reviewing these stories we learn that the creative state can be reached with eyes open or closed. Usually when eyes are open they are defocused (not focused on a specific object). And usually this is done in a relaxed position. Scientific research informs us that the *meditative level takes place at an altered state of mind*... "Altered" meaning different from our "normal" conscious awareness.

This altered state may best be explained by speaking of the change in our brainwave frequencies. Using an electroencephalograph to measure the electrical activity in the brain, we find during the Beta or waking state in the *adult* that the brain produces a pattern (or electric pulsations) of twenty cycles per second. When we go to sleep, our brainwave pattern cycles up and down several times a night — from the waking state of BETA (20 to 14 cycles per second), to the ALPHA level (14 to 7 cycles per second), down into THETA (7 to 5 cycles), down to deepest sleep DELTA (5 to 1 cycles)... and back up again to begin the cycle again and again, three or four times a night.

An "altered state" is anything below wide-awake Beta (*below* 14 cycles). *Meditators* usually function between Alpha and Theta (14 to 5 cycles), but most often at Alpha. The secret of meditation is to hold your awareness at this twilight level of half-awake, half-asleep... called *Alpha-thinking*. The closest state which most of us reach *without training* is "daydreaming."

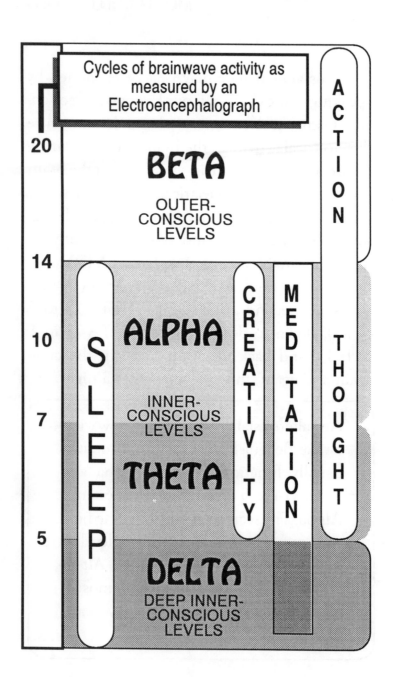

Cycles of brainwave activity as measured by an Electroencephalograph

20

BETA

OUTER-CONSCIOUS LEVELS

14

10

ALPHA

7

INNER-CONSCIOUS LEVELS

THETA

5

DELTA

DEEP INNER-CONSCIOUS LEVELS

SLEEP

CREATIVITY

MEDITATION

ACTION

THOUGHT

Although anyone can learn with practice to meditate, the simplest way to achieve awareness and *control* over the inner-conscious is to take one of the two major training courses — *Transcendental Meditation (TM)* or *Silva Mind Development*. TM is based on a two-thousand-year-old system derived from *yoga* and teaches the quieting of the mind. Silva, based upon yoga, psychology and modern research, uses the *altered state* for more specific purposes — which includes not only quieting the mind but also *directing* thought to problem solving and creativity. Both systems have millions of participants. Silva, the largest of the two, is taught in 87 countries and translated into 18 languages. (For more information read *The Silva Mind Control Method* by Jose Silva and Philip Miele; also *Silva Mind Mastery for the '90s* by Drs. Tag and Judith Powell.)

POSITIVE-ENERGY VAMPIRES

The natural energy high of young children today is too often, and unnaturally increased by the sugar in candy, soda and processed food... which keeps them running at high gear, in a state of constant nervous motion. The older child is *upped* by sugar, rock and rap. Both age groups are *then sapped of energy* by planting themselves in front of the big square black box. The violence on the "tube" is a constant pumping of *adrenalin* into their young sensitive systems. This overload causes short attention spans, nervousness, irritability and a general lack of patience — in short, a great mass of misdirected energy. The parent-solution is two-fold:

STEP ONE. On the Outer Level you can cut down on the bad foods and negative TV (but not all at once, for too rapid a cut-back would send them into withdrawal symptoms just like going "cold turkey" from coffee or cigarettes would us!). Cut back on the constant barrage of negative messages from the violence of film and TV — because this vast and all-pervasive *Negative* acts as a *Positive-Energy Vampire*... which sucks/saps/drains away your child's natural positive energy!

STEP TWO. On the Inner Level you can fill the vacuum created when you cut out those negatives by giving your children *the positive mind of meditation*. The consistent practice of this mind-enhancing technique can be used to direct and channel young energy into creative action. Even more *positive* is its effect when practiced by the whole family, together or individually.

CHILDREN ARE NATURAL MEDITATORS

An interesting fact is that unlike the adult who functions during the waking hours primarily at Beta, the child — until reaching puberty — spends a large amount of their day hours at the Alpha level. Consequently, it is much easier for a child to learn to maintain the meditative Alpha level than it is for an adult. And if properly trained, children can carry this ability through the difficult years of puberty and on into adulthood.

As in all our exercises, meditation should be "fun." You and your children should sit in comfortable chairs next to each other or place your chair beside their bed — but there is a better chance of them maintaining *awareness* if sitting up in a chair. Instruct your young ones that you are going to take them on a Mind Adventure... which next time they can go on alone. You are going along for the first time to lead the way. As you guide this Mind Adventure, *you will find it most effective if*

*you too close your eyes... relax... and let your imagi-
nation go along.* Use the following script for just an
outline as you lead your children into relaxation...
and on into meditation. For the older children,
have fun using your imagination and adapt the
script to suit them.

MIND ADVENTURE TO THE MAGIC FOREST

*Close your eyes... Relax... Take a deep breath
while I count slowly to four... (slowly) one... two...
three... four... Let it out slowly while I count to four...
one... two... three... four... Take another deep breath...
(slowly count) one... two... three... four... Exhale
slowly... one... two... three... four... Take one more
deep breath... (slowly) one... two... three... four...
Exhale slowly... one... two... three... four...*
*Today we are going on an adventure walk through
the magic forest and meet some friendly animals. We
are wearing our favorite clothes for a woodland adventure (describe them to heighten sensory awareness). Let's start by walking across the soft grass of a
green field just bursting with yellow and orange flowers... When we look to our left we see thousands of*

winking, bobbing yellow flowers... the sun is shining so brightly... On the right as far as we can see are thousands of shimmering orange flowers... look way off into the distance... see how far your eyes can see... Take your time... think about how far you can see...

As the breeze blows lightly, you can feel it on your cheeks... you smell the delicious aroma of the flowers... You look ahead and see that the flowers are parted by a path of red flagstones worn smooth by many feet... many happy people have came this way... You see far ahead to a large expanse of forest... You notice some tall trees with dancing silver-tipped leaves... as you skip happily down the stone path you notice the trees seem to get bigger and bigger as you get closer... As you get closer to the forest you notice the tall wisps of green grass under the trees with wild flowers of every color beckoning you forward...

The forest is just up ahead now... you can hear the birds singing in the trees... walk quietly now so as not to frighten the animals... I have heard there is a baby deer in there who won't go closer to the edge of the forest than ten trees... You have to be very quiet for it's only a baby and it startles easily... Now silently count the trees as you walk by... slowly and quietly... one... two... three... four... five... six... seven... eight... look for the baby deer... nine... ten...

Be still, don't move... take a quiet deep breath... exhale slowly... there's the baby deer... with its white spots and tan coloring blending into the forest... you didn't see it at first... Quiet... it sees you ... don't move... take a deep breath and quietly breath out... look at its little nose and long ears...

It's coming toward you... be still and very quiet... slowly put out your hand, palm up toward the baby deer... Now the deer is licking your palm... it tickles... you reach down and pet the baby deer... it rubs its head against your leg... it likes you... It might be afraid of ordinary people, but not you... it wants to play... It runs down the path and then turns and runs back to you... signaling for you to go deeper into the forest with it...

Now the deer is walking beside you... rubbing its head against you as you walk... Up ahead you see a clearing... and an old log surrounded by large white mushrooms... On the tree stump is the biggest, cutest squirrel you have ever seen... The squirrel says, "Hello"... Yes, the squirrel talks... You say "hello" back. "What is this place," you ask the squirrel.

The squirrel starts to tell you about this magic Indian circle, a place where you can escape to, and have fun with all the forest creatures when you just want to get away... or a place where you can come to *find answers when you need them... The squirrel or one of its friends will always be there to help you when you need it or when you just want to talk... Sometimes you may meet the baby deer's daddy or mommy... both are very wise in the ways of the forest... And maybe you might be lucky enough to meet the old Indian chief or the wise medicine woman... but there will always be someone here for you...*

Just remember, when you come again to the forest, pass the ten magic trees that guard the forest... you must silently count them, one to ten, so they'll let you pass...

Now it is your turn to talk to the squirrel or the baby deer... silently think the words and they will silently answer... take your time... talk with them about the Indian Chief or Medicine Woman, or about the other friendly animals who live in the magic forest. Enjoy the friendly quiet of the forest (allow about three minutes of quiet time)...

It is now time to leave this magic place, but you may return any time you desire... to discover many new wonders you haven't even thought of yet... Going back through the forest, you come again to the magic trees... and now you suddenly understand that their names are the numbers... and you have to think their name-number in order to pass... Going out, the trees are backwards, so the first tree is named Ten... as you think his name you reach up and feel his bark... Nine... Eight... Seven... Six, has a bird's nest in her hair... Five... Four... Three... Two... One...

Think goodbye as you move out of the Magic Forest... You feel as if you are floating across the flower meadow... You smell the flowers... Now slowly take three breaths, exhaling slowly each time... one... two... three... Return to the here and now... open your eyes and smile at the world around you!

SUMMARY

Encourage your child to go on a Mind Adventure every day, and on their very own. Be sure to emphasize that these adventures should be done at a special time each day... never during school or while riding a bike or roller skating... or during anything that requires their full attention!

Help them to understand they may seek fun and adventure... or discover new ideas... or solve almost any of their problems during their MIND ADVENTURES.

CHAPTER FOUR

CHILDREN AND THEIR FRIENDS, THE PLANTS

*S*he liked playing in the dirt. Unlike her perfect sister Deborah, Little Patty loved to climb trees or dig dirt or watch little things like ants and doodle bugs — but most of all she loved watching little buds grow into beautiful flowers. She was called a *tomboy* and often came home after an afternoon of play covered from head to toe with dirt, and rips and tears in her clothes. Her sister was the pride of the family, the little princess. Her sister was always perfect in speech and manners and oh-so-beautiful. Neighbors said hello to Patty, but they stopped to chat with Deborah. Patty felt alone and cheated. Although she thought her parents loved her, she knew they loved her sister best.

Patty was only two years younger, but the two girls seemed years apart. Deborah felt that Patty was an obnoxious brat. Patty, as she drew further and further apart from the family, did some foolish and desperate things as a last bid for attention. This caused an even greater gap. Patty's only friends were her "disgusting bugs and her weeds," as Deborah called them. It was not too surprising that Patty had trouble sharing her love of little growing things with her sister.

As Patty grew, even though she was every bit as beautiful as her sister, no one ever told her so. And the other kids made fun of her. She was just too different. She even looked different. Because she was so hard on clothes, her parents had finally given up and let her wear overalls and big shirts. Because she never tried to do anything with her hair, it just hung in a drooping pony tail. Patty truly believed she was ugly. So she became a loner, talking only to her plants and all the other creatures of Mother Nature.

Everyone said Patty had a green thumb — "all of her plants did so well." In fact, every plant she touched seemed to come alive. She had quite a large garden in the corner of the yard but none of her plants, not even her flowers, were allowed in the house "because she made such a mess."

Many of her plants were given to her by neighbors who said "the poor things are dying." To Patty, the plants were people who needed saving. In fact, they were better than people for all of her plants listened to her and usually they would do what she told them to. That's how she knew the plants loved her as much as she loved them. If a plant was growing at an awkward angle, Patty would tell it to straighten up and, sure-enough, within a day the plant would straighten up.

As she grew older and still a loner, she never had successful relationships for she had never learned the rules. Still believing she was unattractive, that no one could really love her, she went into one disastrous love affair after another, never trusting it or anyone since she knew she didn't deserve love. Her only true friends were still her plants.

She had gone on to college, received a degree in Horticulture and now made her living with plants. Unfortunately, to keep a job she had to work with people, which to her was still a problem. Patty today is a very attractive woman... smart, witty... but she doesn't wear a drop of makeup since she believes it's of no use, that she is a failure at life. Unless something happens to her, Patty will spend the rest of that life alone with her plants. Good for her plants, bad for humanity... as she has so much to give.

What can we learn from Patty's story? The important thing for us to remember is that we all search for love, some in very different ways than others. We are all so alike, all part of the greater whole... though each of us walks to a slightly different beat of the drummer. Yet because we chose to see the *differences* in others instead of the similarities, we have a tendency to classify one another.

Most people fall into our so-called range of "normal" behavior and "normal" appearance. A few seem to stand out from the others, to "sparkle" like diamonds. Still others are not like the "normals" or the "sparkles" — they spend their time alone and do things that seem very different, even strange. We often look upon these people as radicals, misfits, nonconformists, "odd balls" — and try to stay away from them, and would like to keep them out of sight. Sometimes we even lock them up.

We praise the "sparkles" and damn the "differents." TV and Hollywood are aglow with "sparkles;" we choose the "sparkles" as our models. Do you the "normal" feel dull and drab around a "sparkle?!"

Now the trick is, to look for the sparkle... and *find it* in your child. You being a "normal," have and probably do play favorites. Come on, admit it. Realize it and then set about finding that special sparkle in the child you favor *less* — because that child marches to a beat too different? And the "favorite" shares your view of the world? Follows your model? Of course it doesn't mean you love the "misfit" any less, but it does mean you tend to polish your "sparkler" a bit more. So think about what you can do to polish and make "sparkle" each of your children!

Now back to Patty: her Green Thumb was more than just an escape, a defense against the world. *Green Thumbing* is actually a little-recognized psychic talent. A talent she unknowingly developed because of her loneliness... and like most young people who develop their innate psychic skills without the support and understanding of their family, it made her even more different and alone. But this particular psychic strength just happens to be the Mother of all the psychic powers. It is truly the mightiest force in the Universe — for it is the limitless power of Love.

As a parent you can help your children learn to channel into *all* areas of life on this planet, appreciate all living creatures. You can help them to develop their own uniqueness. With your support and nurturing, *each* of your children can grow into a loving, confident, successful adult.

The following exercise not only enhances a special love bond between the parent and the child... but it also demonstrates the mighty power of Love in a concrete way that even the littlest child will understand.

LOVE AND PLANTS

Have you ever noticed how some people will touch a plant and it will flourish?... while others, maybe yourself, can just touch a plant and it will die? It may surprise you to learn that plants feel, react, even "think!" And that they develop what could only be called affection for certain people. This has been demonstrated by many scientists and researchers, particularly Cleve Backster.

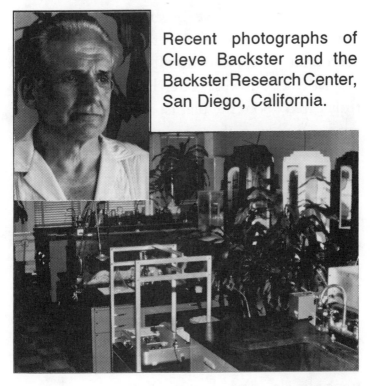

Recent photographs of Cleve Backster and the Backster Research Center, San Diego, California.

As many will remember, Cleve Backster was featured in the book and film *Secret Life of Plants*... in which actual footage was shown of plants responding to the commands of researcher Backster.

The commands were not just verbal — he was able to get a reaction from the plants simply by mental command! Yes, *plants respond to your thoughts.* Think kindly on them.

The key to working with plants seems to be the very essence of Love. Several scientists tried to duplicate the Backster experiments: some were successful, others were not. It is apparent that the *positive* reactions were gotten by the scientists who truly cared about the plants; and the negative response was from those trying only to conduct a study... with little regard for the creatures.

One of the experiments done by Cleve Backster demonstrated clearly that plants have "feelings": they showed distress at the very thought of being cut or burned! Using a Psychogalvanometer, which measures electrical resistance, Backster found that the plants registered a *change*... "registered a fear?"... when he or one of his researchers merely *thought* of damaging a plant. The thought alone was enough to set the plant into a frenzy of electrical change! (You can read more about Backster's work in the new book *The Secret Life of Your Cells by Robert Stone, Ph.D.)*

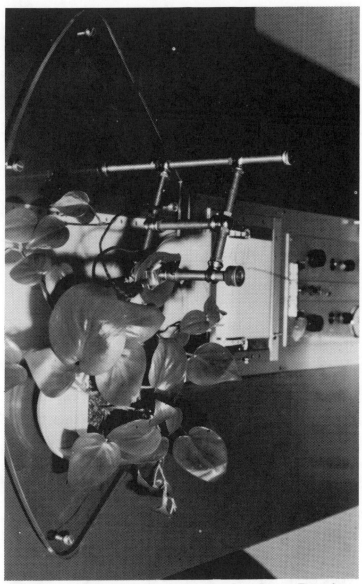

Backster research plant, "hooked-up" to a Psycho-galvanometer, shows "distress" or a change in electrical resistence at the *thought of being burned.*

PLANTS ARE AFFECTED BY MUSIC

Research done by Dorothy Retallack at Temple Buell College, Colorado, suggests that plants also respond to music (as some of you with house plants and stereo systems may already have discovered). During one study, three identical terrariums of plants subjected to three different types of music responded with dramatic differences.

The first group — subjected to Led Zeppelin acid rock music several times a day — grew very slowly and developed only short roots and small blossoms. The second group — subjected to classical Bach music — developed large roots and large blossoms, larger than would normally be expected. The third group of plants did the best — they were subjected to Ravi Shankar (New Age Music) — and developed *very* large roots and extra large blossoms (to see more photos of these experiments get the book called *Sound of Music and Plants* by Dorothy Retallack). You may wish to experiment with your own plants using different types of music.

ROOTS AFTER TO EXPOSURE TO MUSIC

ROCK MUSIC
LED ZEPPELIN

CLASSICAL MUSIC
BACH

NEW AGE TYPE MUSIC
SHANKAR EAST INDIAN

Retallack research plants show various growth rates from exposure to three different types of music.

URI GELLER SPEED-GROWS SEEDS

Uri Geller and his children, Michael and Katherine.

Recently, while we (Tag and wife Judi) were doing mind-training sessions in Athens, Greece, our friend Uri Geller demonstrated even further the power of thought and energy on plants. To show this, he opened a pack of common flower seeds and dropped a few in his palm... then gave the rest to us for experimentation. Within *seconds* the seeds in the palm of his hand began to sprout! In less than five minutes his seeds had sprouted and grown to about half-an-inch high... As far as we could tell our seeds remained dormant.

While most children will not be able to make seeds grow as fast as Uri Geller, we will now show you how to teach your children to speed-grow *Mung Bean* seeds.

HOW TO BRING OUT/DEMONSTRATE THE LOVE POWER IN YOUR CHILD

The easiest way to demonstrate the LOVE power and its effect on plants is with Mung Beans. These beans may be obtained at your local supermarket, or your nearest Natural or Health Food store. Ask for Mung Beans for Sprouting. (By the way, Mung Bean Sprouts are great tasting in salads and sandwiches, so be sure to eat some of what you grow. Backster's research showed that plants enjoyed being eaten, for then they became a part of your *Life Form*! Just tell the plants they are going to be eaten and thank them for their nourishment. This is a more direct form of saying *Grace* — you thank the *food* for becoming a part of you!)

For your child's experiment, get two identical wide-mouth glass containers (mayonnaise jar?) to be the Growing Jars; and two identical quart-size glass Water Bottles (large cola or soda *glass* bottles with a screw-on cap would be perfect). We say *identical* because we want to try to keep the experiment as "scientific" as possible.

For the Growing Jars, you will need a couple of large rubber bands and a small section of cheese-cloth (usually available in the produce or cooking section of your supermarket; or you can use one layer of old *clean* pantyhose.) There are several Bean Sprout Grower Jars on the market you could buy — but your glass containers with cheesecloth, plus rubber bands to hold the cloth on, will do just fine.

You need to distinguish one Growing Jar from the other, one Water Bottle from the other — so use a Magic Marker or a grease pencil to put a big "L" on the side of one of the Growing Jars. Now mark a big "L" on one of the Water Bottles.

A. Fill both of the quart-size Water Bottles with water; fill both at the same time, from the same tap or water supply.

B. Have your child take the Water Bottle marked with the big "L" that stands for LOVE. (A quart of water will weigh just over two pounds and may be a bit heavy for younger ones to hold to their foreheads. The best bet is to set the bottle about twelve inches from the edge of a table — and, sitting comfortably, you and your children take turns *placing your foreheads close to but not touching the "L" Bottle*, with your chins resting on your hands atop the table).

C. Now *imagine* projecting Love Energy from the center of your forehead into the water. Imagine that you can see the water becoming clearer as the Love Energy cleanses and purifies it. Imagine the water *changing and vibrating* as you project the Love Energy. You and the children should take turns of about 10 minutes each. Desired time: 20 to 30 minutes total.

D. Put one teaspoon of Mung Beans into each Growing Jar—be careful to make the amounts equal.

E. Cover the beans in each Growing Jar with about one inch of water from each Water Bottle. *Be careful* that the water from the Water Bottle marked "L" should go into the *appropriate* Growing Jar marked "L" — and the water from the Unmarked Water Bottle should always go into the Unmarked Growing Jar.

F. Place a piece of cheesecloth over the top of each of the growing jars, held in place with a large rubber band. If you don't have any large bands, ask for a few at any Post Office; they use this size to bundle mail and in most cases are happy to give you some.

G. Both of the Growing Jars should now be put away in the cupboard for overnight. Be careful to keep the jars *and* the water bottles away from the light — so be sure to close the cupboard door.

H. *The next morning* pour the water out of both Growing Jars — the cheesecloth will act as a strainer. (Some people drink the water because they believe it has special vitamins and minerals). Gently tap the cheesecloth to remove any seeds that stick to the strainer.

I. Have the kids praise the "L-jar" Mung Beans. Tell them how much brighter in color and plumper-looking they are — but most of all, tell them how much you all love them. Do this even if the "L" Mung Beans do not look any different; use the power of *imagination*. See in the mind's eye, bigger, plumper beans. As for the Unmarked Growing Jar of beans, other than pouring off the water each morning try to have as little contact and emotion about it as possible. Be sure to keep both Growing Jars away from the sunlight, and afterwards always remember to place both Growing Jars back into the cupboard out of the light.

J. *Each night* before your children go to bed, take out both Growing Jars from the cupboard and cover the Mung Beans in each with about an inch of water. As usual, pour the Unmarked Water into the Unmarked Growing Jar... and the "L" Water into the "L" Marked Growing Jar. Again, for about 15 to 20 minutes you and the kids send Love Energy to the "L" Mung Beans sitting in the water. Both jars of beans will be soaking in the water during that "energizing" time.

K. Now pour off the water from both of the Growing Jars and put them back in the cupboard and close the door.

L. This process, Steps J and L, should be repeated for three days, morning and night. Other than the draining, covering with one inch of water, soaking for 15 minutes, and then draining again — no other attention should be given to the Unmarked Jar. The "L" beans — in addition to the watering, soaking, and draining — are to be given 20 to 30 minutes of Love Imagery every morning and night.

M. After the third day, compare the Mung Beans in the two jars. You and the kids will be amazed at the difference a little Love makes! Now taste the difference. Which ones taste sweeter? and juicier? Enjoy the Mung Beans on a salad or sandwich. Remember, they will enjoy becoming part of your entire family's Higher Being.

You and your children may not make the seeds grow quite as fast as Uri Geller did, but you will certainly cause speed-growing in the *loved* Mung Bean seeds!

EFFECTS OF LOVE-VERSUS-HATE ON MUNG BEANS

Not long ago Tag did this experiment with a classroom of children... a class consisting equally of boys and girls from seven to twelve years of age. The only difference in this experiment from the above — we had the kids send 15 minutes of Hate to the Unmarked Beans, as well as the 15 minutes of Love to the "L" jar.

Which of the Mung Beans do you think grew bigger? If you think the "L" beans won as they did above — you are wrong! The beans that were Hated grew *much* bigger! Why? The answer lies in the *innocence* of the children. First, they really knew and understood nothing about Hate — when they tried to project the Hate energy they would make all kinds of silly faces and everyone would laugh and giggle. So the Hate jar got lots of what really amounted to *fun positive energy.* Second, when it came time to send the Love energy the girls did okay, but the boys said "Love, UCHK!". They wanted no part of that "Love stuff" so they really gave little energy to the "L" beans.

Besides being an amusing experience, we learned two major lessons from this: *One*, that Hate is a learned emotion and unless children are trained to Hate, they think Hating is silly. *Two*, boys need to learn it's okay to say they Love something and someone. As the parent, what message are you sending to your children?

SUMMARY

The jury is in — scientific research conclusively shows that animate objects can "show emotions" about the thoughts we send them — and seeing is believing. Do the Mung Bean experiments... and practice on the plants at home. Buy your child a plant of their own which they may keep in their bedroom — and talk to it without feeling silly. Have your child ask the plant what kind of music it likes! Your children's ESP abilities can flourish together with the plants with whom they communicate with — both verbally and mentally.

The mind connection that everyone may have with plants can also be nourished when working with animals, such as the household's cat or dog; or iguana or snake! Teach your children to love all things and creature, big or small.

CHAPTER FIVE

THE CHILD AS A HEALER

*D*ony was an eight-year-old with sparkling blue eyes and hair the color of the sun. He was an average active boy with one small difference — his parents had told him that people had the power to heal each other by transferring energy from their hands. He was still at the age where he trusted his parents... and besides, he had experienced his daddy's "magic touch" that stopped the bleeding when he fell out of bed one night and got a bloody nose. His mother had always stopped the pain when he hurt himself — but of course everyone knows that's "mother's stuff"... all mothers can do that. He called this healing touch the POWER HAND.

One day, his dog Fang wasn't well. Fang, in spite of the name, was a very loving and kind German Shepherd and was Dony's best friend (unless you counted his imaginary horse who lived in the woods behind the house). Before leaving for school he found Fang softly crying, dragging both back legs... they seemed paralyzed. His parents called the veterinarian, but could not get an appointment until 4:00 P.M. Sadly, Dony trudged off to school, worrying about his dog. At lunch he rushed home with an idea — why not use the Power Hand to help Fang? His Dad said, "Sure, why didn't we think of that!"

Dony ran out the back door to the big tree, Fang's favorite spot. Fang looked up at him, crying, his legs stiffly stretched out behind him. Dony dropped to his knees and placed both hands across the hips of his beloved dog. He closed his eyes and sent Fang's hips the love energy his folks often talked about. After about one minute, Fang let out a *yipe*, stood up and began licking Dony's face. He ran out about ten feet and then back. Fang's legs were okay again!

At four o'clock, Dony and his parents took Fang to the veterinarian for his appointment. Upon close examination the vet could find nothing wrong. He said that German Shepherds often had hip problems, but he could not account for the paralysis going away like that. At any rate, Fang was now in good health. Dony knew from that day forward that his Power Hand worked!

After that momentous day, one would often find Dony playing happily in the yard... healing beetles and lizards and frogs, and even a bird! Being a typical boy he got more than his share of cuts and bruises — and took great joy in being able to instantly stop the bleeding and make the pain go away. His bruises rarely lasted more than a day as he would use his Power Hand to make them disappear.

A few months later, Dony's parents received a note from his school requesting a special parent/teacher conference. When they arrived for the meeting, they were met by four of Dony's teachers. It seems a little girl was hurt during play and Dony volunteered to use his "Power Hand" to help the child. He closed his eyes... "to get the power started," he said... and then touched the crying little girl's arm. Her pain stopped. The little girl wiped her tears, moved her arm and said "it doesn't hurt anymore" and resumed playing.

This was all but forgotten by Dony and the little girl, until after recess when another student brought it up in class. He reported to the teacher what had happened. One of the children then asked the teacher to explain how Dony could stop someone from hurting just by touching the spot with his hand.

This event was the reason Dony's parents were being asked to come to school. The teachers (for word had certainly spread) wanted to find out why Dony thought he could heal others. When the parents explained that Dony *was* a healer, and could use his energy to speed healing and reduce pain, the teachers had mixed reactions.

One teacher said she had heard about such people and wanted more information. Another said she knew some people could do healings and did not see anything wrong with it. The third said there was no such thing as the ability to heal by touch and the boy should be taken to a psychiatrist to remove his delusion. The fourth said he was an instrument of the devil and should be exorcised.

After much discussion it was agreed that Dony should perform no more healing on school property.

Later, Dony complained to his parents that a teacher was making fun of him, telling the class how Dony's parents had made up the story of the Power Hand... so all the children began laughing at him and calling him names. Even though his Healing Hand could instantly stop bleeding, cause rapid healing and remove pain in others, Dony used his skill less and less until his belief in the Power Hand and its effectiveness disappeared. One little note of interest: the paralysis in Fang's hind legs never returned.

The Power Hand, as Dony called it, or the "healing touch" is easy to teach anyone — but it seems that children gain greater control, and faster control, than adults. The real problem is to instill a *lasting* belief in their abilities and prepare the child for the doubting and ridicule of others. In a later chapter we will cover the complex problem of *confidence*... and how to confidently continue using one's psychic gifts from childhood on into adulthood.

THE HEALING TOUCH

The process is most effective when we can start the training from birth. Yes, from birth. When your child gets the little bumps and has the falls that all children get, it's best to treat them with laughter and love rather than alarm. Even if it scares you, smile and laugh at the hurts and cuts. Always tell the child that the touch of your hand will make the hurt go away and make the cut heal faster. As soon as your child understands that your touch makes the hurt go away and the cut stops bleeding and closes up, you will have instilled the *belief* of the healing touch... and that activates the child's natural healing mechanisms.

The next step is to show the little ones how to heal their own bumps and bruises. Always ask them to show you how successful they were. Smile and praise them on how well they got rid of the hurt and helped speed the healing. This not only builds confidence in their abilities, but allows you to see if any other action should be taken about the injury. Yes, we certainly do believe in standard medical practices and treatment, in addition to the healing touch. In many cases the little problems can be solved at home — but be sure to *always* examine, with a smile, *any* hurt or pain and make a decision if additional medical treatment is needed.

It's best to practice the following experiments alone and in advance... to gain more confidence in your *own* abilities. It is important to remember that each person is different and may *sense* things differently. Your children's experiences will be slightly different from yours. Most likely their *sensing* may be more acute, more intense... as they have not had years of negative programming to hinder the feeling, the awareness of these special energies. You, of course, will never give them negative programming... or hardly ever.

THE ENERGY BALL

Explain to your children how we have an *aura* or energy field or life force that surrounds our bodies. To explore this we are going to play catch with an Invisible Energy Ball.

We suggest you practice this exercise first and then as the teaching parent you'll be better able to guide your children. You are going to take the energy from all around you in the air... and compress it down into a small ball of *pure energy*.

Put both hands in front of you as if you are holding a beachball about *three feet* in circumference. Now bring your hands together, fingers curved... as if you were holding a Softball of about *four inches*. With a deliberate pulling condensing motion... bring your hands in from the three-foot ball to the four-inch ball... as if compressing the Beachball to the Softball... and then expanding it back out again to three feet... and then in again.

Imagine you can feel the energy building in the four-inch ball each time you bring your hands together. Shape the Energy Ball, feel it, feel the tingle... when you can feel the four-inch Energy Ball, *toss it* to your children. Ask them if they could feel the energy coming toward them... could they feel it when they caught the ball? Ask what it felt like. Be sure not to describe your own feeling as theirs will probably be different from yours.

Now have each of them build the Energy Ball... guide them in compressing the energy from the air, from the large ball into the smaller ball. Guide them to do just as you did earlier. Tell them to take their time... until they really have that energy compressed enough to hold together when they toss the Energy Ball. When they *feel* it is ready... have them toss it back to you. Did *you* feel the Energy

Ball coming... when you caught it? What did it feel like? How did your experience differ from theirs?

This activity is a fun exercise to do in a group of *any* age. You can sit in a circle and toss the Energy Ball to each other. It makes a great party game!

"SENSE ENERGY COMING FROM THE HANDS" GAME

Find a quiet place and sit in a comfortable position with your hands resting, palms up on your lap. Close your eyes and take a deep breath and relax your body. Starting at the top of your head... pretend that each part of your body is relaxing as you breathe deeply, slowly. Continue to relax your body... going down down down... to the tips of your toes. Continue to breath deeply.

Rub the palms of your hands together rapidly for about 10 seconds. Rest hands, palms upward on your lap. Notice the warmth and tingling in your palms. The friction caused by the rapid rubbing does two things to help us sense energy: first, it removes dead cells on the surface of the skin, making the hands more sensitive; second, it stimulates and increases the blood circulation.

Rub your palms together again for a few seconds... now hold the palms *facing* each other, about an inch apart. Feel the energy flow... and describe the feeling.

Repeat the rubbing and again hold them about *one inch apart*. Notice the feeling... and now move the palms about *five inches* apart. Notice and qualify the difference. Now move the palms back to *one inch* apart. Notice different feelings at different distances.

Some individuals identify the difference as a change in warmth, a change in pressure, an increasing tingling sensation or vibration – any feeling is correct, just different interpretations of the same phenomenon.

Rub and repeat the testing, with your palms at different distances. If you lose the sensitivity feeling (tingling feeling), just rub your palms together again. As soon as you can really feel the difference in distance, you can practice *without* rubbing your palms together – this greatly enhances your sensitivity awareness.

You will shortly be guiding your children in the "rubbing of palms" game... guiding them in

Rare energy photo: Dr. Judith Powell and her new Scottish Terrier puppy, *Master*, the Enlighted One. Note the energy coming from the right hand.

experiencing the energies... allowing them to interpret the energy in their own words... helping them develop a powerful healing touch. But first, let's understand a little more about ENERGY.

You are becoming aware of, as well as detecting, the body's natural energy. Your body produces most *different* energy fields — which can be measured by standard equipment. Examples of this are: your heat radiation aura which can be photographed by an infrared camera; your electromagnetic field which can be measured by electromagnetic meters — and this static field aura can actually be recorded and plotted by computers!

Some scientists believe that it is the *special particles* in your body's electromagnetic field that are *the actual energy source used in healing.*

"FEEL THE AURAS" GAME

The best place to start is with the head, for several reasons; it is one of the most highly energetic areas of the body, and therefore, is the easiest area to feel. Place your child's hands close together, palms downward, about two feet above the subject's head, who will be sitting in a chair. Have them slowly, lower their hands until they feel "resistance." Tell your child to avoid actually touching the subject. You want them to feel energy, not the physical body. If they don't seem to feel anything on the first pass, have them do it again. If they have developed their sensitivity with the previous games, they should pick up the feel of the aura on the first pass. As always, however, if at first they don't succeed, encourage them, and do it again.

ENERGY FIELDS AND KIRLIAN PHOTOGRAPHY

Now let's try some scientific talk about Energy and the *Kirlian* Photography process:

Kirlian Photography can be used to show us how we unconsciously-consciously *modulate* the flow of energy coming from our bodies... how our thoughts, our emotions can modulate that flow. But the Kirlian process, often misunderstood, does *not* measure the *natural* energy coming from the body — an *outside* energy source must be introduced into the body in order to photograph the *electrical flow*. What the Kirlian process does do is allow us to measure and record the changes in "The Gates" — the resistance or lack of resistance at specific points in the body. The Gates allow the outside electrical energy to leave the body... or to enter it.

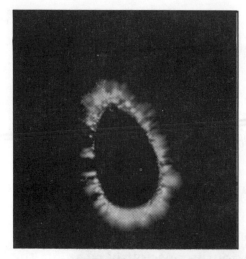

Kirlian Photo of fingertip energy Gates, subject is at normal outer-conscious state (producing Beta b r a i n w a v e activity).

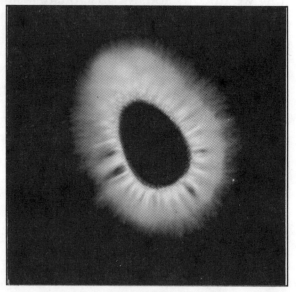

Kirlian Photo of fingertip energy Gates in Healing mode. The subject is in their inner-conscious state. This is the subject's meditative\healing mind-set (producing Alpha brainwave activity).

> *The Kirlian process photographs the amount and locations (Gates) of the release of that external electrical energy, plus the Kirlian aurora and the color changes in that aura/ energy, as the energy leaves the body.*

This research with Kirlian Photography demonstrably proves that when we are in a *relaxed state of mind* our Gates are most open to an exchange of energy... with another being.

This research also suggests that the use of Visualization can increase the flow of one's *natural* energy from the Gates.

So why all this scientific gooble-dy-gook? To emphasize the importance when *healing* of maintaining a relaxed state of mind. To understand that when *the sender* places their hand for healing the hurt or the cut... they will be more effective if they can *visualize* or imagine the hurt going away, the cut healing.

It is also important that *the receiver* be in a relaxed state... as this allows their Gates to be open to *accept* the healing energy. Furthermore, having the receiver of the energy imagine the pain leaving or the cut healing... will help to *direct* the healing energy to that critical location.

WHO HAS THE POWER?

There are as many different healing methods as there are healers, and most have merit. (We are speaking, of course, of genuine healers, not the fakes or frauds.) To say one is better than another is not only unfair, but inaccurate. For the *power* lies in the *mind* of the healer, not in the method. If you *believe* you can heal, you have "stronger" healing power than a person who believes they can't.

Dr. Bernard Grad at the University of Manitoba, Canada, successfully demonstrated that *everyone* has the healing gift. In one experiment he took a group of white mice and made a small identical cut on each one. He divided the mice into three groups. Mice of Group One (the control group) were treated only with proper food and water. Mice of Group Two were healed with "LAY-ING-ON of hands" by a professed healer. Mice of Group Three received the "LAYING-ON of hands" from a student lab assistant (copying the movements of the professed healer) who said he had no healing abilities.

The results were dramatic. Group One mice, the control group, healed in a normal expected time and fashion. The wounds of Group Two mice, "healed" by the healer, did indeed heal very rapidly. But the mice of Group Three, the student's group, healed faster than the control group, but not as fast as the "healer" group. This experiment shows us that the *physical* healing energy is present in all humans... that the *difference in power lies in confidence and in the mental processing*. Remember, there was no "receiving" imagery attitude in the mice — so you *can* cure that wounded frog!

STEP-BY-STEP LAYING-ON OF HANDS

For your first time at this, the healing will work better if you sit in a comfortable chair and relax your body... as you have been doing in all the exercises. By now you should be familiar with the relaxed feeling and be able to call on it at will.

Think of being at your relaxed "center" — that place of personal peace, where you can be in contact with your Higher Power. After more practice, you will be able to quickly reach this state by simply thinking of how it feels to be there. Later, out in the stressful world, sitting at your desk, standing in a line... you will be able to close your eyes and simply think of being at your Center.

Now *visualize* a Golden Light of Love entering your body from above. Imagine the feeling of love and peace as the light enters your head... imagine it flowing into your entire body... from your head down, down to your toes. This "filling-of-the-Spirit," or rather, this filling of the body with the *Spirit*, may be done slowly to enjoy the experience. Later, when you want to (or need to in that stressful world!) you can experience the "filling" in just a second.

Now direct the Golden Light into your Right Hand... and hold it two to three inches *above* the area to be healed. This hand gives *out* the energy. Now take your Left Hand... and place it *below* the area to be healed. This hand receives the unhealthy, bad energy. If not convenient, place your Left Hand to the left of the affected area (next to your Right Hand). For general healing or just to give more energy to your subject, place your Right Hand above the thymus gland (mid-breast-bone area) and your Left Hand above the upper back area, between the shoulder blades.

Now direct the *healing energy* flowing from the palm of your Right Hand into the troubled area... and mentally pull the problems and the negative energy into your Left Hand... so that it will flow up and out, and out of *your* body. *As you are only acting as a channel for the flow of energy, there is no chance of you keeping any of the subject's (person needing healing) problems or pain.*

As you imagine the Golden Flow of energy coursing through the subject, visualize the problem disappearing and the person becoming healthy. Your last thought should be of that person in perfect health.

Now remove your hands from the subject, and put them together for a moment to allow the Golden Flow to course through *your body...* to cleanse and heal you, the healer. Use this moment to reflect on giving thanks for this gift of healing.

After you have practiced these techniques, have the joy of teaching them to your children. Because this could be considered "serious stuff" by some adults, be sure to keep it FUN lessons for them... and keep the sessions SHORT. Always be positive and keep praising any results, any at all. Look for the things done right and praise them highly.

In recent years, the Healing Touch has had the benefit of much scientific research and validation. Dr. Dolores Krieger has, for many years, taught and lectured at some of the nation's top medical schools, including New York University — training literally thousands of doctors, and especially nurses to use the healing touch.

Author of *The Therapeutic Touch*, Dr. Krieger is thoroughly convinced that the ability to use Therapeutic Touch is a natural potential within each of us, which can be actualized under the appropriate conditions. Her methods include centering oneself, "unruffling the energy field" (aura), directing and modulating the transfer of human energy (thought and color energy).

SUMMARY

Whether it be to soothe a cut or a bruise, relieve a headache, alleviate a muscle spasm or calm a crying baby, you and your children can develop the Power Hand. Recapture a simple ancient mode of healing — laying-on of hands. Show your children how they can become an integral part of their own healing process, and your's too. Take the concept of taking away the hurt with "a mother's kiss" a step further... reach out — touch and heal someone!

CHAPTER SIX

PSYCHOMETRY: OUR SECOND SIGHT

A mother was going through some old jewelry when a ring fell to the floor. Her daughter Beverly, a quiet little girl, with deep almost hypnotic brown eyes, quickly scooped up the ring... examined it and then returned it to her mother.

"Whose ring?" Beverly asked. "Your Grandmother's?" was her mother's reply. "I thought so," the little girl said, almost talking to herself, and then went on, "but Grandma was only a young girl when she was given that ring." Amused and a bit curious the mother asked, "That might be true, but how do you know?"

"Well... it's just stuff you know when you hold something... and you know what else? that ring was given to Grandma by a boy with white hair." At this point the mother was startled, because it was an engagement ring given to her mother by her first husband at the time of proposal. She was even more surprised when she suddenly recalled that her mother, who had said little about her first husband, had mentioned that his hair was the palest blond that she had ever seen, almost white.

"Okay. What else do you know?" the mother asked, handing the ring back to her little Beverly. The child held the ring between her clasped hands and closed her eyes. Shutting her eyes helps her think, she later told her mother.

"Grandma is fourteen years old and lives in a house with many rooms and floors. She has her own little garden where she grows vegetables and flowers. And her parents couldn't afford electricity for lights so they had to burn gas, use lanterns and candles to see at night."

Beverly's mother was taken aback for she knew her mother had just turned fifteen when she was married, and she did have a flower and vegetable garden. Her mother's house *was* big, with three floors plus an attic. But the clincher was the detail about the lights. It was not that the parents couldn't afford lights — when her mother was a teen, electricity was only in the downtown area and the lines were not run to her parent's house until several years later, so of course they used gas lights and occasionally kerosene lamps and candles!

Little Bev was able to see all this because she had the gift of what some people call "second sight," or more specifically, *Psychometry*. Fortunately for Bev, she had an understanding mother who fostered her daughter's natural abilities, helped her develop into a secure, well-rounded adult. With this confidence, Beverly was able to expand her vision to encompass many other ESP talents. Today she is a well-known psychic and a consultant to many important people.

> *Psychometry is the ability to gather specific information about a material object or structure... by merely holding the object in your hand, or touching the walls or any part of the structure/ building.*

Think a moment — have any of your children ever picked up an old ring or necklace and begun to talk about the "original owner" when they had no idea who it ever belonged to? Of all the psychic senses, Psychometry is the one which relies on the *physical*, the sense of touch... and may be the perfect example of the body/mind/spirit relationship. The outer sense of touch is one of the first senses to develop, and is the primary data-gathering tool of the young. Remember when your children were going through (are still going through?) that phase when they just had to touch everything? *Touch* allows their eager brains to add a physical realm to their bottomless pit of ignorance about life on the earth.

Now let's see if we can help you, the parent, develop that special "know by touching"... close your eyes... and touch the paper of this book. What do you feel? Paper, yes, but what do you *feel?* Since you normally take a page-in-a-book for granted, you tune out the data about it... just as you tune out the data about most everything you touch, everything around you... you take it for granted. You have desensitized yourself to "fine data"... because over the years you have decided what is important and what is not, so you filter out information you do not consider "useful."

Let's try the paper-touching again. Move your fingertips lightly back and forth over the paper. Notice whether the paper is smooth or rough, warm or cool. Other than this, you will probably not get much more data out of the page. Your sensitivity is *adult-dull*, but your child just might be able to pick up more.

A child might notice the tiny wood particles in the paper or feel the small changes of its thickness, or feel the warmth of the ink, or... something more.. The feel of sunlight as the seed bursts forth life that will form the tree that the paper is made from... or feel the grasp of a bird's claws as he hops along from limb to limb.

Far-fetched? A bit much? With the play of the psychic senses who is to say how far is OUT?

So let's see just how "far out" it is: back up for a minute and lightly press your fingernail into the paper of this page. Note how your nail left an impression in the paper. That impression of your nail is there forever. You compressed the paper, and regardless of what happens to this book, the change you made in the surface of the page made changes down to the molecular structure of the substance. Your compression changes the molecular vibration. If we could follow the atomic level of the nail imprint we would see that if this book is recycled — or God forbid, burned — the compressed section will be minutely different in the pulp, or in the ash! There is nothing that does not put forth its own unique and particular radiating vibration, its specific energy pattern — and that pattern remains, inviolate.

One example: by using a process called *Carbon-14 Dating*, archaeologists can learn the age of an artifact thousands of years old by simply measuring the amount of radiation it gives off. As we know from high school physics, matter can neither be created nor destroyed — just transformed.

So changes in matter at any stage can be recovered in that structure which formed a specific pattern that is never lost, just transformed.

Our quest is to become sensitive enough to pick up the transformed pattern and reconstruct it into usable data. The young have not yet amassed the negative blocks which would prevent the unfolding of this.

The next few games will help your child to develop the sensitivity needed for Psychometry. As with all these PSI or psychic skills, you can use the games/experiments to develop your own abilities as well, but the children will be your best model — for they will learn much faster!

"FIND THE PHOTO" GAME

This ability is one of the most popular games in Tag's psychic children's classes... and the accuracy of the children has been amazing!

Begin by having your children sit in comfortable chairs and relax... by taking three deep breaths. Now, just like before, ask them to rub the palms of their hands together until they tingle... to sensitize the surface of the skin and allow for easier reception of the psychic energy. The tingling is similar to the feeling that many get when using their healing skills. Furthermore, when a child performs a known function like rubbing, it builds a feeling of fun and anticipation. This, again, is a step in Sensing Energy, so necessary in Psychometry.

You will need for each child a set of six *identically-sized snapshots*. It would be best if they were all processed at the same photo processor (to keep the reverse side of the photos the same in appearance); better yet, if they were all processed at the same time. Each snapshot should be of a *different person or object* (pictures from the same magazine will do just fine).

It might be fun, and certainly helpful, to shoot the sets of photos... at a party or picnic. In each set, *two* of your PSI photos should include a picture of the child (laughing, smiling... having fun), and *one* photo of a favorite relative, best friend or pet — someone or something to which your child has a *strong emotional attachment*. The remaining *three* photos in each set could be other people they know... and even objects.

Besides the basic set of six for each participating child, shoot several more sets of six each — which include snapshots of you, your spouse, your home, the TV, your child's room, the kitchen or dining room... and any building, room or place that your child can easily identify, such as the school. Of course, these are just suggestions, so feel free to photograph anything of special interest to that child. The main point — keep each photo limited to one person or one object; not to have a lot of extraneous objects/people.

We're ready to "play." Have the children sit at a table of comfortable height. Now place before each child the six photos of his or her set *face up* so that the child may view them. Point out particularly the photos of themselves and of their favorite relative, friend or pet. Then pick up the *photos* and with your back turned so that the child cannot see — mix up their order, and this time deal them *face down* in front of the child. Be careful your young one doesn't peek.

Ask each child to lightly rest a fingertip on the back of each photo... sensing the energy... to "locate" the picture of themselves and also of their "favorite." When these *two photos* are "selected," ask the child to move them forward (to separate them from the other four)... and then have them sense the energy of these two photos again... to tell which is themselves and which is the "favorite."

By "sensing" and "selecting" two out of the six photos, the odds of probability of correct selection of at least one of the two are increased... which will greatly build their confidence when they choose correctly.

Now put down a different set and ask them to find a *particular* person or object. Depending on the number of photos you have to make sets out of, you can continue to "play" the game. Now make up a new set... consisting of the most successful "selections" (the correct hits) from the original sets. We suggest that you do no more than six rounds all together... or else the children could get bored. Always keep the games SHORT so that it's easy to maintain interest and promote fun with PSI games.

And naturally, we all tend to "pick" the photos of people, places or things to which we have the strongest emotional attachment.

Remember, you are developing sensitivity... and what you are asking your child to do is really quite fantastic. Be sure to keep a light casual attitude and praise the "hits" and make light of the misses, or better, forget them altogether.

This game is not meant to be a scientific test of psychic abilities as are conducted by J.B. Rhine at Duke University — it is meant to be something much more important: *developing*, not testing, your child's PSI. And a positive fun game attitude is vital. Once the child feels any pressure to be "right," stress enters and it's no longer fun — and *you've* lost the "game!"

After playing the Photo Game a few times, your child will have developed a sensitivity to receiving energy from inanimate objects. Now they are ready to move into classic Psychometry!

WHY DOES PSYCHOMETRY WORK?

An object of any kind — a ring, a glove, a book, a car! — absorbs and retains the impressions of the emotions, the happenings going on around it. In detecting the impressions from a piece of jewelry, your child may "flip" back to the mining of the gold, the fashioning of the article or, even more so... to the time when the jewelry was worn by a particular person. Like the physical impression of your nail on the paper, the thoughts and feelings of that person or persons have vibrations which leave impressions on everything around them (you *know* houses have vibes!).

To "read" an object, we must rely on our inner-conscious levels to give us usable information, information that we can interpret. An object which has strong emotional ties to the owner or previous owner will be most effective for this exercise.

In future years, we may find it possible that impressions or vibrations retained by an object may form symbols which act as *keys* to open obscure information banks. Some will call this data source: the *Super-Conscious*, the *Universal Mind*, *Akashic Records*, or *God*. Look to whatever name of the "source" which is the most acceptable to you. Your child may as yet be free of these names... and will therefore be more open... to success.

THE PSYCHOMETRY GAME

Have your children relax... taking three deep breaths... exhaling, inhaling, slowly slowly... while holding an object in one clasped hand (such as a stone, a leaf, a cup, a ring). They should sense the vibration... the tingling or different feeling in that hand. Suggest to them that they ask themselves just what thoughts they are having (not usual everyday thoughts)... to say anything that comes to mind... the *first thing* that comes to mind.

If nothing comes, suggest they let their imaginations wander over the object, *into* the object. To let themselves feel whatever they might feel if they just really let themselves. In this first game, tell them it's okay to *pretend* or even *make it up*. Because if they take off the wraps — the information may come fast and furious and in abundance, so much so that it is a good idea to have a tape recorder on hand to get it all down.

The first few Psychometry "readings" may be just the child's imagination but as the stress of "trying" dissipates through repeated game-playing, the accuracy can improve dramatically. It's also possible your child may be producing accurate information on the very first try, so don't disregard anything! How are you going to know if it's accurate or not? Because for some strange reason, you get a tingling all over. Like something "up there" is saying, bravo!

Don't be concerned that you're telling your child to "pretend" or even to make up an answer. Remember that the *imagination is the doorway to PSI abilities*. The thoughts out of imagination are from the inner-conscious level... the level of inventing, discovering, creating! This may be the Open Sesame to those *inner data banks.*

This concept of "data banks" could explain why so many inventors, discoverers, theorizers — have come up with the same idea in different parts of the world at the same time. Several examples are: an English inventor named Joseph Swan and an American inventor called Thomas Edison — both came up with the electric light bulb at the same time. In fact, Edison and Swan formed a company to jointly manufacture the bulbs. The telephone was invented by Alexander Graham Bell in America and Elisha Gray in England at the same time, only Gray registered his invention two hours after Bell had been granted his patent. And of course that most famous "coincidence" of all — Charles Darwin and Alfred Wallace, an unknown British naturalist working in Malay, were simultaneously working on the theory of the origin of species! The secret of genius seems to lie in the "sensitivity" of a few to receive or access information missed by the many.

"FEEL HOW THE LIGHT VIBRATES"
GAME

For this game you will need a small penlight or small high-intensity flashlight. You want a small but bright light with a close, tight beam. A lamp, lantern or large flashlight will not do because it generates too much heat — and that will give away the answer, and the PSI-developing game.

Have your children hold both their hands behind their backs, palms out. Shine the light on either the right or the left hand. Now ask each child to guess which hand the light is shining on. Ask the young ones to *mentally see* the palms of their hands behind their backs and decide which hand *looks* the brightest. Have them wiggle a finger of the hand which has the light shining on it. The wiggling of the finger prevents the children from getting confused over which is their right or left hand!

SUMMARY

You can understand now how Psychometry can be another and possibly better way to gather data in a confusing world. Where we just don't have enough outside data. Psychometery is interesting, fun and useful (crime-solving!). So use it, be more decisive — and enjoy!

CHAPTER SEVEN

METAL BENDING

*H*e was only six when strange things began to happen. Enjoying a bowl of his mother's
wonderful onion soup, the spoon in his hand
began to bend... just below the bowl on the stem
part, it slowly began to bend. The boy froze in
amazement. The soup dribbled down the front of
his shirt and into his lap. He watched as the spoon
continued to bend, until it broke in half and clat-
tered on the table.

If this happened to you, and you were only six... what would you do? How would you feel? His parents were no help since they weren't even there to witness it, and of course didn't believe "it just broke by itself!" They didn't believe him for a long time... until he became an embarrassment because this uncontrollable spoon bending began to happen several times a month. His watch would move forward in time of its own accord — the hands of his watch would even bend up! Who could he talk to? His parents, busy with their own problems, tried their best to ignore it; teachers wouldn't believe him; other kids would just laugh and make fun of him saying "it's all a trick!"

I am sure you have guessed by now that the young boy was Uri Geller. Why did his powers manifest when they did and so out of control? Of course we will never really know, but Uri said this was during a time of great family stress. His father was away from home much of the time and his parents, whom he loved dearly, were discussing a divorce. Maybe this outburst of psychic energy was his unconscious crying out in emotional pain for attention, or maybe his inner-conscious was trying to pull his parents' attention away from *their* pain... or maybe it was a desperate attempt to hold his family together.

A CHILD'S ENERGY

The Energy of the average child is astounding — if you measure the size of the child against the energy output! But this natural vibrancy of early childhood too often becomes dissipated, lost as the child grows — sometimes lost through a decreased intake of nourishing energy-producing foods with an increased intake of fast foods, snacks and chemically-hyped instant dinners.

Even more to blame: the energy-sapping of a barrage of *negating* that a growing child undergoes — from parents, teachers, siblings, the neighborhood kids... in general, the world. Such negative feedback can produce a state of ennui boredom, why try? Or rather, why bother? *inertia* in the child. But this negative feedback does more than just impair a child's natural physical energy (as if that weren't bad enough!). It impairs, and can cancel out, the energies of the psychic plane... one's inborn PSI abilities, one's special "gifts."

We take for granted (and often forget) our psychic talents when we "grow up" and become adults. We become stronger, run faster, fight harder and generally (with "luck") reach somewhere near our potential. In short, we usually leave our willess, ignorant, helpless, weak, effete, *powerless* childhood behind. Not so! There is one place where the child (if "unimpaired") proves to be vastly superior to the adult — and that is in the world of Psychic Energy. We've just seen a prime example of that: the spoon bending.

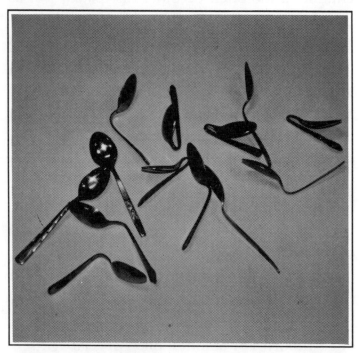

A few of the spoons bent by the children attending Tag's recent workshop.

SPOON BENDING

In workshops Tag and Judi conducted around the world, they have learned that *children* can bend spoons in one quarter the time that it takes an adult — and some of the "grown-ups" can never bend a spoon at all, at least not with just their minds! Most children can bend a spoon... using only their mind-power... in five to fifteen minutes. It usually takes an adult forty-five minutes to an hour to bend a spoon, if at all!

The common explanation for the difference is "belief." Adults have years of negative programming and "know that the mind cannot change the molecular structure of metal." Children in their innocence "don't know any better," so they can bend metal easily. This is one factor — but we should also consider the compacted strength of the psychic power within the *young* child... a power still happily unimpaired by the negative world of "you can't." A power untapped because too often nobody knows it's even there. If it is seen there, too often it is *denied*. When the world around denies, the child refuses to believe.

Most children still live in the super-world with Superman and Wonder Woman, Teenage Mutant Ninja Turtles and Teenage Atomic Kung Fu Chickens. Most children still believe that they too can do marvelous feats, if someone will only show them how. Or if some child does do a marvelous feat, *don't deny.* Let that child be "marvelous."

So let's teach the kids how... But first, why bend spoons? Is there something special about a spoon? Not really. A fork or knife can be bent as easily but a fork has sharp tines and a knife has a cutting edge — therefore, let's use spoons.

What type of metal? Any metal can be used although we rarely see the parents giving their children the good silver for the spoon-bending class. The most common and probably the best for this is *cast* stainless steel. You can pick these up at any Flea Market or Goodwill shop. (When you buy spoons for this exercise, be sure to buy extras so your children will not later show off their newly-found abilities with your good flat wear.)

Beware — don't buy the cheap *thin-stamped* stainless steel because the spoons will bend too easily — and your children will wonder if that

Teenagers and youngster at a 1992 workshop.
The one young lad was the first to bend a spoon.

bending they see was really done with *their* minds!
Or worse, they don't wonder and, full of "success," they try it later... on regular cast stainless
steel. You guessed it. Failure. A very disappointed
and possibly embarrassed child. Just one more
way to damage inner confidence in themselves, in
their developing PSI abilities. So remember to
buy the thick-cast stainless steel spoons — and
many of them for future bending experiments!

HOW TO BEND SPOONS

A relaxed atmosphere is the key to any psychic experiment. Have the children seated on comfortable chairs, eyes closed... take several deep breaths, exhaling slowly... and have them relax their bodies into their chairs. If you have already taught them meditation techniques, ask them, with spoon in hand, to enter their Center; the altered state of conscious-awareness... their Alpha level. If they are still using the Magic Forest Metaphor (see Chapter Three), have them imagine sitting on the old tree stump with the animals as their audience watching as they bend the spoon. Select a spoon for yourself to demonstrate with and do this along with the children, they will probably bend their spoons long before you bend yours.

When you believe the kids have reached their state of inner-awareness (and children do this very quickly), tell them to open their eyes... and slowly, closely examine the spoon... starting at the handle, noticing the bottom and the top of the handle. Now direct their attention to the neck of the spoon, just before it widens into the bowl. *This neck area is the focal point for our energy transfer.*

Children's mind development class, 1980

Now tell them to hold the spoon with the bowl extended and facing up, with the back of the neck resting on the first joint of the index finger. The rest of the handle will be cradled in the palm of the hand, with the other three fingers wrapped around the handle. From this position they should be able to rub the front of the spoon's neck with their thumb. Now tell them to put their thumb in the bowl to *lightly* test the strength of the neck by pressing on the bowl, while the first finger continues to support the neck. This will give your children an idea of how strong the neck is, to notice its degree of flexibility.

Tell them: "*Rubbing the neck of the spoon between the thumb and first finger, imagine the metal getting soft... from the friction and heat generated by the thumb against the metal. Imagine that this heat is enough to change the molecular structure of the neck of the spoon to make it become soft, almost as soft as lead. As you continue to imagine and to rub the spoon lightly, you will notice the neck getting warm.* (You know this heat is simply caused by the friction between the spoon and your fingers.) *Imagine the heat flowing through your fingers, through the metal... down into the atoms of the metal... the internal heat rising, making the neck of the spoon softer and softer... making it bend like soft putty.*

"*Now test the softness by checking the bowl with your thumb with just a slight pressure... note the resistance, the stiffness... soon it will become soft as lead, bending easily like play-dough. Continue to rub the neck of the spoon... imagine it warmer, changing, softer, more flexible. Project your special energy through your fingertips to make the neck of the spoon become softer and softer.*

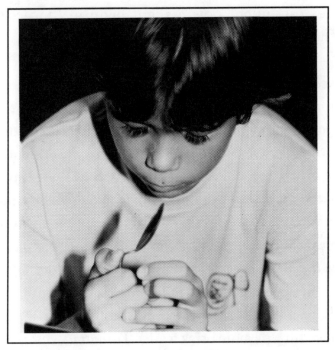

The moment of truth! Photo taken as the spoon was bending.

"*Now with your thumb in the bowl, check your progress...*" (give them time to test). Your children may find the metal becomes soft, starts to bend — and then, suddenly stops. This sudden hardness may be because their logical mind reared up and told them it's not possible to melt metal with nothing but your mind and your fingertips! Have the children test the metal stiffness with their thumbs. Though they may find it hard and stiff, they just might note a slight bend in the neck. Then they know that it *did* become soft!

"*Continue to rub the spoon with your fingers, feeling the heat returning... projecting your energy through your fingers... and as you rub, you notice the spoon getting softer and softer... feeling the metal changing to soft lead or to putty or clay, just as it did before. When the metal begins to feel like soft warm putty, check the flexibility again with a slight pressure to the bowl with your thumb. Notice how the slightest pressure causes the spoon to bend... more and more as the metal becomes soft as putty... softer and softer as the spoon continues to bend. You may again feel the metal suddenly get hard* (suddenly, as if you have hit a psychic brick wall!). *Throw out, cast them away, those negative "logical" thoughts... and continue to rub and bend the spoon. Believe in your own power. Now be careful not to rub too hard or the friction will cause blisters. Keep the pressure firm but gentle.*"

How do we know they're not applying so much pressure during the testing periods that their fingers, not their minds, are bending the spoon? The answer is simple: examine the bend. A forced-pressure bend will cause a sharp, almost right-angle bend. A mind-power bend (supplemented with finger-friction until your mind can do it alone!) will be almost a perfect curve, a rolling round arc. The exception: if you used one of those cheap thin-stamped spoons we warned you about. Even with mind power in most cases they bend sharply, not roundly, because of the thinness of the metal.

SUMMARY

The mind is a powerful energy tool — and you don't even need a plug! We have seen children bend spoon handles into perfect circles to make rings for themselves. This is something you could never do with fingers alone. We have seen spoons bend up, others twist lengthwise, and one where *the bowl* bent in the middle! It has been reported that a child in California even bent a railroad spike!

Adults also bend spoons. At one of our recent metal-bending workshops, Judy Denchfield, editor of *New Awareness Magazine*, bent a large serving spoon — over a quarter-of-an-inch thick, and one-inch wide at the neck!

CHAPTER EIGHT

ASTRAL TRAVEL

*J*oan was about three years old, playing in the backyard with her sister... when she suddenly became aware that she was looking *down* on her sister playing below. At first the feeling was of awe, and then the feeling turned to panic... as she realized she was floating in the air about 50 feet above the ground. Joan called to her sister for help, but her sister couldn't hear her. She screamed for her mother to help! She could see her mother down the lane talking to a delivery man. Then, just as suddenly, Joan was back on the ground. She tried to explain to her mother what had happened. What did her mother do? Her mother washed the "lie" out of daughter's mouth with soap.

Joan was confused, this strange happening seemed so real. Even though she was only three, she vowed to herself never to tell anyone else about the event... if not even her own dear mother would believe her.

But the strange experience didn't stop there. At night in her bed, if she began to think about what had happened, she would find herself "journeying." As she grew a little older and more accustomed to it, she would give herself up to the sheer joy of this feeling of free-flight. Joan began experimenting by projecting herself to the strangest places — once, out of curiosity, to the inside of a camel's stomach! Not very pleasant. YUK! but certainly quite a test of her small-child abilities. She was trying to figure out just what limits this strange power had, this free-floating go-anywhere talent within her.

As Joan grew into adolescence, she found it safer to shut down her "trips" because no one would understand her or this strange energy. The busy outer-world was now beginning to demand too much of her. But being a teenager, and wanting to "connect" with others, she broke her vow one time and tried to talk about her adventures with "friends." They, being adolescents, thought she was crazy. No more friends.

Years passed with no events. Then on a family camping trip during her senior year in high school, atop Pike's Peak in Colorado, she had another "happening." She had wandered off to investigate nature... and on a large rock, lifting her arms toward the heavens in sheer joy at the beauty spread out before her, it happened. Without warning... just as it did when she was a child. There she was, suddenly, air-borne, floating over this majestic wonder. To her, reveling in the scene from such a unique vantage point, this was an experience to top all those in childhood.

Best of all, now, as an almost-adult, she knew this was not a child's dream or an imagined fantasy. It was real. A special gift that others did not seem to have or even believe possible.

As the years passed, she would "fly up" and watch the neighbors mowing their yards, view the townsfolk scurrying about, see children at play in the park.

Sometimes she could sense the emotions of those closest to her; this was not always a pleasant feeling. Friends, acquaintances thought her odd — too distant. And, sadly, this special ability began to complicate an already-failing marriage.

Joan is just one more case of the lack of understanding of such gifts... causing fear and frustration in childhood, a feeling of isolation in adulthood. The stress of keeping these powers a secret contributed to years of unhappiness for Joan. Only much later, with the raising of her two children who were also "gifted," did she find peace with her natural talents.

A clue to whether any of your children have done *Astral Traveling* can be an innocent remark such as "last night I visited Aunt Marie." Although this comment may be just your child's healthy imagination, it would be a good idea to listen to the story of this visit to Aunt Marie. Even if the "trip" was only a dream, the recalling of the dream can be very productive. Remember our talking about Robert Louis Stevenson and his "Dream Elves"?

To discover if your child did make an honest-to-gosh Astral Trip to Aunt Marie, ask encouraging questions. By having a positive and non-judgmental attitude, you can reinforce the *joyful* use of Astral Travel and direct your children in this fascinating "gift." If you are one of the many adults who have difficulties accepting the reality of this, at least know that *exercises in both Astral Travel and Mental Projection will help your children expand their creativity, their imagination and visualization abilities – which, as you remember, are the key factors found in every genius.*

WHAT IS ASTRAL TRAVEL ANYWAY?

It is the ability to project oneself over a distance to another location. This, like any other PSI talent, is a *natural* function of the mind.

Probably the best way to teach your young ones to experience, and have fun with Astral Travel (and not fear it... like when they suddenly feel themselves "taking off" and don't know what's happening!) is to begin by dividing the phenomenon into two separate functions: Mental Projection and Astral Travel.

Although some experts differ in their definition of the phases of Astral Travel, we've made a working distinction:

> ✻ Mental Projection is the projection of the MIND to a distant location... so that you will be able to see (or know) what takes place there.
>
> ✻ Astral Travel is the projection of our physically-sensing ASTRAL BODY to a distant location... so that you will be able to not only see, but to feel the conditions there, as if you were physically present.
>
> ✻ Mental Projection is often the first step to Astral Projection. Often not — sometimes one just takes off!

The ability to do Mental Projection first manifests in what we call a *daydream*. Think of what happens in a daydream... you blur your vision and suddenly find yourself living a different reality. It may be a simple recalling/reliving of the past... or it could be seeing/thinking of something that is happening to someone else in a distant place... or it could be seeing/experiencing something happening in the future.

Have you ever noticed how real some of your daydream trips seem to be? How you can recall an incredible amount of detail? What people are wearing, what they are doing, even the paintings on the wall? It's possible that your daydream was more than that, that it was actually Mental Projection.

For most of us, we daydream without much control. Our minds seem to wander off, possibly to escape boredom... or an unpleasant situation. When we become aware (or someone else makes us aware!) that we are daydreaming, we usually snap abruptly back to the here-and-now. Then we've lost any information that it might have been trying to get through to us.

Often, when we try to daydream on demand, as in an Exercise (or trying to escape?), we have difficulties. As for your children — it would be a good idea to teach them to take *control* of the daydreaming process — to do it deliberately, in off-hours, and not in class! That they should do it when they need to think creatively, to find solutions to a problem — and not when they should be listening to a teacher saying something they may need to know.

Although we can daydream standing up, sitting down, or in almost any position... adults may find the control of it enhanced by relaxing the mind and the body. (Of course, we are *super*-relaxed when we unconsciously/unknowingly daydream!) So to practice this exercise, to gain that control... and to take the first step toward Astral Travel, you will, as in all the PSI exercises, relax the body and the mind. Remember, children spend much of their waking time at the Alpha level already, so it will all be easier for them.

By now you are familiar with the basic procedure of the relaxation "script"... and know the magic is not in the words but in the doing... so feel free to *ad lib* as you see fit, to suit the age and temperament of your audience. As long as you stay within the general idea, you can loosely follow this format for the rest of the Mental/Astral Travel Games.

THE MENTAL PROJECTION GAME

Tell your children to go on this Mind Trip, they will begin by lying on their backs... or sitting in a comfortable chair. *"Now close your eyes and take those three very deep slow breaths... relaxing your body while inhaling and exhaling... slowly."*

You will be asking them questions about things you want them to notice. For now, they will answer only in their minds... and then later they can tell you all that they have noticed after you all finish the "trip."

"*Think of your body relaxing, all the way from your head to your toes... down... to your toes... (Give it time)... Now that you are relaxed, imagine your body slowly, slowly rising... up into the air... Imagine the ceiling above you getting closer and closer as you rise into the air... Pretend you can see the ceiling... What does it look like up close?... Now reach out and touch the ceiling... What is the texture, is it smooth or rough?... notice the color... Now you are floating out of this room and into your own.... look down upon your room and notice what you see... look at your bed... Is it made?... Notice the color of the sheets or of the bedspread... Look at your desk or your dresser... What do you see on top?... Notice everything, is it messy or tidy?... Notice anything in the room that has color or special texture, your clothes or the rug... Now move out of your room and return to where you are, returning to your body... (pause). Take a deep breath and exhale slowly... open your eyes... look around... you are back.*"

Now ask your children to recall *everything* they saw. Ask them to pay close attention to the smallest detail. When they are finished describing their "trips," ask them to get up and go to the bedroom. When there, ask them to check all their "hits" — the things that are exactly as they described on the "trip."

Ask if they *touched* anything while "traveling" in the bedroom. Sometimes Mental Projection will turn into an Astral Trip if they *feel* something, have physical contact with something during the experience. Do not press, allow this to occur naturally and unfold at the child's pace.

In the beginning, we use the words "imagine" and "pretend"... to keep the logical mind from fighting the Mental Projection. After one "trip," you should be able to give instructions matter of factly... never asking IF or CAN YOU. This positive approach *presumes* success. Also note, we used a location known well to a child. Since they can easily recall most of the information asked for, it acts to prime the pump or to start the flow of data. And it builds their confidence... for those "trips" further out!

Remember, it is absolutely essential that you keep all the PSI games stress-free... and fun. Repeated successes can almost be guaranteed if you stay away from the "misses" or incorrect answers, and concentrate on the "hits" and correct details they recalled. Any positive experience in these games helps your children feel more certain of their abilities. If the children begin to tire of the game, it may be that you have not made it entertaining enough. Or you may be going too slowly. Or you may be pushing too hard. At any sign of boredom, stop the game immediately... and next time make it more fun!

MENTAL PROJECTION GAME TWO

Our next game is to project to a location *outside* of the house, to a place the child is familiar with and enjoys. Guide the "trip" as before... this time adding more details by asking these questions: "*How does the temperature feel?... Is it warm or cold?... What sounds do you hear?*" Be sure you keep the questions casual and short; use them to trigger the children's curiosity and tune up their sensitivities.

MENTAL PROJECTION
GAME THREE

This time you will guide your children to visit a relative or friend they like — maybe Aunt Marie! Be sure the "visit" is to a living person. The first two games were for the purpose of seeking out and identifying only articles, things — unless the children on their own had decided to make it a "people trip."

Follow the same format as above, then tell your child: *"Let's go visit Aunt Marie... Is she at home?... Let's see what room she's in... What's she doing?... How is she dressed?... Is Aunt Marie alone?... Is the radio or TV on? What's playing?... Is it cool or warm in her room?"*

Ask questions that require your child to use the senses of sight, sound, smell, touch and taste. These will gradually take the child from Mental Projection to Astral Travel... because with this third sojourn, they are definitely on their way!

MENTAL PROJECTION GAME FOUR

The kids should now be ready to solo — to go on their own! As before, as in all the PSI exercises, have them relax by taking three deep slow breaths. Now suggest several "trips" they might like to go on, or they may choose places known or unknown for themselves; places they would enjoy (not too far, this first solo trip!). Be sure to tell them to keep their "destination" a secret and not tell you until they get back, and that you will give them plenty of time for their adventure... before you call them to return.

Now send them on their way... allow them their fun time (about half an hour)... and when that time is up, softly call out their names and tell them it's time to come home. Then when they open their eyes have them tell you all about their journey. Ask about everything, all the details — all the senses.

ASTRAL TRAVEL GAME

The kids, having mastered those Mental Projection exercises (leading them into basic Astral Travel) — are now ready to move on to "big-time travel"! The world is theirs — with no worry about reservations or flight schedules. You can stimulate their ideas by cutting pictures from magazines or getting brochures from your travel agent.

Consider this — by using Astral Time Travel, they can enrich (enhance/improve/and maximize!) their school work by projecting to foreign countries they're studying; by going back in history to witness a famous event or see a once great city.

IS THERE A DANGER IN ASTRAL OR MENTAL PROJECTION?

Astral Travel is safe and no harm can come to you or your child while on a trip. Perhaps one time or another you have heard some old-time talk... about a silver or golden cord, or "astral thread," that extends from your astral body as you travel to your left-behind physical body... a cord that keeps your spiritual/mental/physical being interconnected. You may also have heard that if anything breaks this "cord" during your trip, you cannot return to your body and it will disperse/ die. This concept of "cords" or astral threads is an old *occult superstition!*

In all our years of researching and teaching the metaphysical sciences, *we have never read or known of one documented case of harm (or death!) coming to anyone through Astral Travel.* We have had conversations with well-meaning occultists who repeat this old wives' tale as it was taught to them, and who actually still believe it. That's too bad, for it prevents them from exalting in one of the most wonderous of the PSI gifts and, worse, they might "turn off" others who have this gift.

So what *does* "protect" your physical body as you astrally travel? Your mind. Yes, it is your mind that protects you for THE MIND is universal, everywhere... because there is no time dimension or space dimension when you are travelling by "Astral." Your mind is with your physical body as well as with your astral body... so there is no need to fear anything happening to that physical body you left at home in your bed, or "lying under a tree," as the Yogis are said to do. Your mind is *there*, safeguarding the physical body while your mind is *with you*... zipping around the world or in the camel's stomach!

You ask where did this heavy negating come from? In olden days, fear and superstition and half-truths were bruited about, used to control the masses and keep the "power" in the hands of the elite. Today, in the blazing light of modern times, there are still many people who fear the meta-physical, the "super-natural" (which is as natural as Nature herself, just on a higher mind-plane). There are others, sadly, who, lacking confidence in their own PSI gifts, will use this superstition as an excuse... rather than admit they're afraid they have no inborn talents.

SUMMARY

The message is, of course, loud and clear — never teach your child to fear anything ("fear" and "beware" are too entirely different concepts: one hits the unreasoning, emotional, reacting mind; and one triggers the logical, thinking, solving mind). Fear is the most negative of energies, sapping joy from existence. It causes mental stress, even mental decay and psychic disorders. Fear encourages disease, can destroy the body... through the body-destructive emotion of stress.

So instill in your children a respect not only for all things, but all possibilities. If they are raised with an open mind, they have a better chance of living a more balanced and secure and happy life.

Give your child a chance at Mental Projections and Astral Travel — it is a exhilarating, exciting experience. Take a trip for yourself and find out!

CHAPTER NINE

REINCARNATION: WHEN YOU LIVED BEFORE

*S*ome children in their younger years may be heard to say something like "When I was a cowboy...When I lived before... When I was married to John..." These seemingly meaningless words can be from an active imagination, or... they could be coming from knowledge of a previous life.

Because most parents try to stop the child from what they believe to be foolish flights of fantasy, these utterances of what might be a bridge into the past... could be lost forever. By your saying something *very* casual like "Oh, you remember that time?... what else do you remember?... tell me about it..." — keeping it light and very conversational — will allow your child's memories (if they are memories) to flow forth.

Whether you believe or disbelieve in reincarnation, such gentle-talking-with-child can be interesting, even illuminating... for as you might already be aware of, there have been many documented cases of verified past life memories.

Let's look at the life of Michael "Sunny" Lamont, Jr. Little Michael had the good fortune to be born to what would be called enlightened parents. His father, Dr. Michael Lamont, is a noted scientist and international lecturer, a well-known author of a book that has sold almost a quarter of a million copies. Dr.Lamont's research is on the cutting edge of the scientific frontiers of today. Dr. Lamont is also a noted inventor and the holder of many U.S. patents, and works today in the special elements that seem to reduce aging. Little Michael's mother, Dr. Janet Lamont, is also a noted scientist, author and lecturer in her own right.

From the start, Michael was what one would call a exceptionally bright child. And like most babies, he was attracted to bright shiny things, like his father's Rolex watch. In fact, little Mike would cry and not stop crying until his father gave him the watch to grip in his tiny hand. It wasn't too surprising that one of the first words out of the child's mouth was "mine," as he pointed to the Rolex watch. Then again, this behavior isn't exactly unusual.

As he grew older, little Mike wanted to be called "Sunny" and commented that he was a Ray. When his mother agreeably called him Sunny Lamont, the little tyke would say "No, my name is Sunny Ray." Most mothers feel that their children are little Sun Rays and call them by such endearments, so no problems so far.

But young Sunny started talking about "his wife Dawn" and their being together in his other "lifetime." Further, to the complete astonishment of his parents who played classical music around the house almost every day, little Sunny began to show a great love of Country and Western music (before it was fashionable) and would sing along with the TV any time a Country or Western song came on. Most unsettling, he seemed to know the words!

As the years passed, the saga of when Sunny lived before began to be a bit old hat to the family ... until Sunny was about seven.

At that time, Dr. Lamont was lecturing in Texas. After the lecture, he was congratulated by one of the audience who happened to mention her name was Dawn Ray. The coincidence was so striking, Dr. Lamont asked her if she was married. She replied that her husband Sunny "had passed on" about eight years ago. With that statement rocketing around in his head, Michael Senior made an appointment to meet Dawn the next evening.

When they met Dawn Ray, Dr. Lamont and his wife Janet tried to explain to her about little Sunny and his memories of when he "lived before." Mrs. Ray graciously agreed to meet the child. Sunny arrived by plane two days later and was taken by his parents to Mrs. Ray's home; he had only been told there was someone he was to meet. When Mrs. Ray opened the door, the boy exclaimed "Dawn," ran forward, threw his little seven-year-old body into her astonished arms, and gave her a great big kiss!

After things had calmed down, they all sat in the Ray living room listening to young Sunny recalling some of his memories as "her husband" Sunny Ray. Very skeptical at first, Mrs. Ray asked if he remembered this house. The boy said no. Dawn explained that she had only lived there six years, that her husband had passed on two years before that and had never seen the house.

Little Sunny asked, "Do you still have my guitar?" Taken aback, Dawn went to the closet and brought out an old guitar which little Sunny began to play. All watched as the small hands strained across the big guitar to reach the cords. Slowly, hesitantly, a well-known Country song began to be played. Sunny had never taken music lessons nor had he ever picked up a guitar before.

Later on, little Sunny asked for his watch, which Dawn produced from a small box in the closet. Yes, it was a Rolex... identical to his father's. Then he asked for his camera and his pipe, which the adults asked him to first describe. It was quite an amazing evening.

Dawn Ray eventually sold her home in Texas and went to California to live with the Lamonts, and for several years helped raise little Sunny. Dawn later moved to New York to have her own place. Soon afterward, with everyone's permission, Sunny also went to New York and continued to live with Dawn Ray.

At age fourteen, Sunny began a major professional career — a sort of non-medical *Doogie Howser*. Today at only nineteen he is considered a genius in his field.

This is a true story. We can attest to having known the "Lamont" family for many years. Of course, the names have been changed since the "Lamonts" and Sunny want no publicity or interviews. Although the publisher will forward any mail sent to the Lamonts, do not expect a reply.

A complete verifiable past life experience like Sunny's is rare ...and in this book, we are not looking for that kind of regression. We are looking for interesting, exciting discoveries... to keep the door open to the many *future* possibilities of the *past*.

DISCOVERING A CHILD'S
PAST LIVES

Uncovering some past-life memories with your children will be a fascinating adventure for all of you. In the first few sessions the children may seem to be "making it up," since young ones have a natural need to please the parents. However, do not disregard the first few "trips" because, as you now know, imagination comes from the inner-conscious wherein lies truth. As they settle into the routine of the Regression Games, your children will actually begin to unfold more and more of the past.

In Regression exercises particularly, be sure to do them with only one child at a time – for obvious reasons. Experiencing a past life is not like bending a spoon, hardly a group game!

At times the information given by your child can be truly exciting. Remain calm and probe for more. Always determine that your child is in a *positive* past-life experience and be sure that you always suggest a positive, happy time to go back to

— like a party or a Christmas visit. *At any sign of fear or discomfort by young ones, move them forward to a happier time, or bring them out of the session. (See Quick Bring Out.)* Negative encounters can do no more harm than a scary movie. (Scary movies bring on too much of an adrenalin flush...besides scaring their little pants off and giving them nightmares. So if you can't keep this fun, don't do it!)

The Regressions here are designed to help children explore and develop their positive ESP talents — not for negative explorations or to cure fears and phobias. Although many psychologists are doing great work in this field, that is not the purpose here. Your child is to feel confident with many *positive* Regressions — negative, random, or personality-corrective Regressions should NEVER be performed without training or guidance by a professional.

Now that you are ready to begin, it's a good idea to *unplug the phone* so you won't be disturbed. Have your child sitting comfortably or lying in bed (sitting is better to stay conscious enough), with a pillow for comfort and a cozy cover if it's at all chilly. Be sure you too are sitting comfortably.

READING THE REGRESSION SCRIPTS

You might want to read aloud to yourself several times the following exercise (or any of them in this book) when your child is not around... so you will be comfortable and feel natural with the script. If you think it necessary, you may of course adjust it with your own words, but be sure to keep the same basic thoughts and outline.

As you did in the relaxation scripts, read this slowly in an even-flowing tone. When you see three periods (...) pause, slowly take a deep breath, exhale and proceed.

When you ask any question... wait for your child's answer. If no answer is forthcoming, repeat the question. Still no answer? Repeat the question again, firmly and with love. If still no answer, move on to the next statement or question.

If the child answers the question too softly for you to hear, repeat the question and ask that it be answered more loudly. If the answer is still too soft to hear, say "*I am now going to snap my fingers and you will remain where you are... relaxed... with your eyes closed... and you will be able to answer the question louder."* Then snap your fingers and ask again.

LET'S GO BACK TO YOUR BIRTHDAY PARTY GAME
(A basic Age Regression technique)

Now that you are both comfortable, say to your child:

"Close your eyes... Relax... Take a deep breath while I count... (slowly count) *one... two... three... four... Exhale slowly, while I count...* (slowly) *one... two... three... four... Take another deep breath...* (slowly count) *one... two... three... four... Exhale slowly...* (slowly) *one... two... three... four... Take another deep breath... one... two... three... four... Exhale slowly... one... two... three... four...*

"Today is (give month, day and year)... *Relax, as you think of beautiful colors. Imagine the colors going down your body, relaxing the body... Allow the colors to start at the top of your head, relaxing the head... the colors are moving down into your neck and shoulders, relaxing you deeper and deeper... The colors move down into the arms, relaxing... down into*

the elbows... wrists... hands... and out the fingers... relaxing... Now the colors move back up to the neck and shoulder areas, relaxing... down into the chest and trunk of the body, relaxing... The colors move down into your hips... thighs... knees... ankles and feet and into your toes... relaxing your entire body... Feel how relaxed you are...

"As you relax even more, imagine the colors forming a beautiful Color Time Tunnel... Allow yourself to gently float down the Time Tunnel... going down... down... going back in time... Relax... You know that you are a Time Traveler going down the tunnel... notice how the colors change on the walls of the tunnel as you travel back... Each different color on the wall of the Time Tunnel represents a Special Event in your life... During another Time Trip you may explore each color if you wish... This time you are going back to a Favorite Birthday, maybe a special birthday party that you really enjoyed... You are going back to a fun, happy time...

"As you imagine the Special Color representing this special time flowing around you, you find yourself at your chosen birthday... Look down, what are you wearing on your feet? (Wait for answer!)... How are you dressed?... Describe what you are wearing

(Wait for answer!)... *How old are you?* (Wait for answer!)... *Do you know today's date?* (Wait for answer!)... *What is today's date?* (Wait for answer!)... *Where are you?* (Wait for answer!)... *Who is with you?* (Wait for answer!)... *How are they dressed?* (Wait for answer!)... *What are you going to do now?"* (Wait for answer!).

(Ask questions which may seem fitting: *"What games are you playing?... What are you having that's good to eat?"...* ask anything that may bring forth a pleasant experience. Keep this point-in-time interesting. If your child shows signs of tiring or being bored, you should return. Too short is better than too long. Keep the game fun).

RETURNING TO PRESENT TIME

"Look around one last time and tell me, what do you see? ... (Wait for answer!)... *You know you can come back to this particular birthday and enjoy the fun any time you wish... Is there anything you want to do before you return?* (Wait for answer!)... *If not, then it's time to return to your present time* (give today's month, day, year)... *There is a special light all around you now... Feel this light lifting you into*

your Color Time Tunnel... You are floating higher and higher as you move from the past time toward the future which is now... Moving up toward the white light far away up the tunnel... Noticing the beautiful changing colors ... slowly changing to pure white as you move through the Time Tunnel toward the Now... You know soon you will arrive back where I am, at the white light...

"You are now back in the here and now (give today's month, day and year)... *When you open your eyes you will feel wide awake, feeling fine and in perfect health... Open your eyes and smile at the world around you.*"

Using this Regression to a *happy* birthday a couple of times (different past birthdays in *this* lifetime) will help your child relax and grow accustomed to the Time Tunnel and the method. Then you can proceed to honest-to-gosh *Past Life Regression.*

QUICK BRING-OUT

If for *any* reason you need a quick bring-out — someone pounding on the door (put a sign out), phone ringing (disconnect it), pot boiling over (don't cook now), you may use this method:

MIND ADVENTURE

IN PROGRESS...

DO NOT DISTURB
OR
ENTER QUIETLY

Sign for door, you can go to your nearest fast print operation and have a photo copy made for about a dime. They will usually enlarge it at no extra cost. Have several extra copies made.

Call your child's name, softly and firmly, say: "*Relax... I am now going to count from one to three, then snap my fingers... you will return to the here and now, and open your eyes, be wide awake and feeling great... One, two, three* (snap)*... eyes open and smile at the world around you...*"

"WHEN YOU LIVED BEFORE" GAME
(Past Life Regression)

As you did in the last exercise, you might want to unplug the phone and hang an appropriate sign: "*Enter Quietly... Mind Adventure in Progress... Off on a Time Travel,*" whatever suits your fancy. Let your child pick one. Now have the young one sitting or lying down comfortably... with a pillow beneath the head and a light cover against any chill. You too should be sitting comfortably. Now read as before, slowly, in even-flowing tones.

"*Close your eyes... Relax... Take a deep breath while I count...* (slowly count) *one...two...three... four... Exhale slowly while I count...* (slowly) *one... two... three... four... Take another deep breath...*

(slowly count) *one... two... three... four... Exhale slowly... one... two... three... four... Take another deep breath... one... two... three... four... Exhale slowly... one... two... three... four...*

"*Today is (give month, day and year)... Relax as you think of beautiful colors... Imagine the colors going down your body, relaxing the body... Allow the colors to start at the top of your head, relaxing the head... The colors move down into the neck and shoulder areas, relaxing you deeper and deeper... The colors move down into the arms, relaxing... down into the elbows... wrists... hands... and out the fingers... relaxing... The colors move back to the neck and shoulder areas, relaxing... down into the chest and trunk of the body, relaxing... The colors move down into the hips... thighs... knees... ankles and feet... relaxing your entire body... Feel how relaxed you are...*

"*As you relax... imagine the colors forming a beautiful Time Tunnel with a Golden Light far in the distance at the end of the tunnel... Allow yourself to gently float down the Time Tunnel... going down... down... going back in time... While noticing how the colors change on the walls of the Time Tunnel... you know that you are a Time Traveler going back in time... each different color on the wall of the Time Tunnel representing a Special Event in your now-*

life... *(Some other trip you may explore each color if you desire... a favorite birthday or any happy day you desire...)*

"You are now coming to a specially bright Color on the tunnel wall which is the Time Symbol for a special event, your birth in THIS LIFE... the color is so bright it almost hurts your eyes... yet it's a beautiful color... Now pass that momentous time and keep moving down ... going back in time beyond your birth... You feel warm and comfortable as you float down the Time Tunnel... going down... down... down... Enjoy the colors as they change... as you go back to a time and place where you have lived before... remembering you have chosen a color of a happy lifetime...

"You see on the tunnel wall directly ahead of you, the joyful color you have chosen... and you know you have arrived... at that happy lifetime... Now a light, a GOLDEN LIGHT begins to appear in the middle of the color... This Golden Light grows stronger and brighter and spreads throughout the color... and you realize... that the Golden Light is your DOORWAY to your chosen past life.

"Now step into the Golden Light... step through it... and you are there... in another time... a time where you lived a happy lifetime before your birth... Take a deep breath and exhale slowly... (Allow time and watch as the child takes a deep breath and exhales)...

"*Look down at your feet... Are you wearing anything on your feet? (Wait for answer!)... Shoes? Sandals? Boots? Bare feet?*" (Wait for answer!)...

(In many cases, the child in answering may sound faint and far away; if so, ask them to speak up. You may have to ask several times, and always in a pleasant firm manner.)

"*Is anything covering your legs? (Wait for answer!)... What color? (Wait for answer!)... What is it made of? (Wait for answer!)... What else are you wearing? (Wait for answer!)... What color? (Wait for answer!)... Feel the material, describe it (Wait for answer!)... How does it feel on your body? (Wait for answer!)... Are you male or female? (Wait for answer!)... Are you standing or sitting? (Wait for answer!)... Look down at your feet again... Notice what is beneath your feet... Is it the ground or flooring? (Wait for answer!)... What does it look like? (Wait for answer!)... Describe it. (Wait for answer!)... Look now at what is in front of you... Describe it (Wait for answer!)... Look to your left and to your right... Describe what you see (Wait for answer!)... What is above you?... Describe it (Wait for answer!) Who are you? (Wait for answer!)... What do you do in this life?* (Wait for answer!)... *What is your name?* (Wait for answer!)... *Where are you?* (Wait for answer!)... *What are you doing there?* (Wait for answer!)... *Who is with you?* (Wait for answer!)... *How are they dressed?* (Wait for answer!)... *Clench your hand, make a fist... Do you feel strong or weak?* (Wait for answer!)... *Walk toward something and touch it... How does it feel?* (Wait for answer!)... *Tell me more about you in this past lifetime.* (Wait for answer!)... *Tell me about the people you love in this life."* (Wait for answer!)... (This can take a while, probe — see if you are in there!)

(SUCCESS ANCHOR)

"In this happy other lifetime, what special talents do you have? (Wait for answer!)... *What do you do that people say you really do well?* (Wait for answer!)... *You can use this special talent in any of your lifetimes...To help you tune into this talent put your first finger in the center of your forehead, just above your eyebrows, and lightly rub your forehead at this spot... Do this now... Anytime in the future you want to use your special talent all you have to do is to touch this spot with your first finger. This talent will be available to you in all your lifetimes."*

RETURNING TO PRESENT LIFE

"Look around one last time and tell me what you see. (Wait for answer!)... You know you can return to this lifetime when you desire... Just wish to be there... Is there anything you want to do before you return? (Wait for answer!)... Anyone you want to see? Anything you want to say?...

"If not, it is time to return to this present life in the future (give today's month, day, year). Now the Golden Light is all around you... feel this light lifting you up into the Color Time Tunnel... You are floating higher and higher as you move from the past time toward the future which is now... Moving toward the light at the far end of the tunnel... Noticing the beautiful changing colors as you move through the Time Tunnel... Ahead you recognize the special bright color of your birth in (Give month, day and year)... As you pass this light you know soon you will arrive back where I am, at the White Light... Notice the changing of the colors of the Time Tunnel, slowly changing, getting lighter and lighter towards pure white...

"You are now back in the here and now (give month, day and year)... When you open your eyes, you will feel wide awake, feeling fine and in perfect *health... Now open your eyes and smile at the world around you."*

WHY PAST LIVES?

You are asking why all this talk of Past Lives? Why should anyone live, or need to live, more than once? Because, to put it simply (and isn't it painfully obvious to us?), we are all so imperfect, have so many lessons to learn. We must learn first to become AWARE of what we are doing in this life... to ourselves, to others. We need to learn to DO, and to UNDO and do again.

For most of us mortals, depending on our level of consciousness, of AWARENESS, this takes many lives... the doing and the undoing.

Uncovering past lives for us as adults can give more of that awareness. For your children, it can be (and always make certain that it *is*) a fun adventure. It can marvelously tune up their ESP abilities. It can make them more confident, secure, achieving young people... with a feeling of who they are, and even what they are doing here in this family!

Of course, you can use these scripts with other adults. Use them to explore relationships which may be similar in this life as in a past life. WHY we are here this particular time and with these particular people! Discover answers as to why you act or react a certain way, or have a certain physical condition, or even a certain talent... because of something that was learned or existed or happened in a previous lifetime. So use these exercises... for the progress and good of all. We wish you many wonderous learning and growing and becoming lifetimes. God bless!

SUMMARY OF ESP FOR KIDS

ESP FOR KIDS is a book that we felt needed to be written. We hope you will share it with your friends, but we recommend you either buy your friends a copy or suggest where they can get one. Do not loan your copy — for you will discover that this book is rarely returned, even by the most well-meaning! This is a handbook you will use over and over again... at many stages of your and your child's life... to make a difference in the future... in your child's future and the future of this planet. Enjoy and use in good health *ESP FOR KIDS!*

DR. TAG POWELL

Dr. Tag Powell received his Doctorate in Psychorientology from The Institute of Psychorientology, Texas. In the mind development field this is the highest level of certification. He has also earned his Masters and Trainers Certification in Neuro Linguistic Programming.

For over a fifteen years, Dr. Powell has expertly guided tens of thousands of adults, as well as hundreds of children, along the path to becoming happier, wealthier, and more successful people. Some of his workshops include *Spoon Bending, The Taming of the Wild Pendulum,* and *Dowsing for the Young and Old.* He is a living example of what he preaches: that by learning to scientifically train and channel more of your mind, you will improve yourself to your highest potential.

Tag has taught around the world including: The University of Hong Kong, Hong Kong, and The Malaysian Institute of Management, Kuala Lumpur, Malaysia.

He is a favorite of radio and TV talk shows, and at one point, he co-hosted the award-winning cable TV show, "It's All In Your Mind."

His wit and humor provide a relaxed atmosphere at his seminars and lectures, and they are not to be missed. Winning the Silva Method's Presidents Cup as the Best Lecturer in the United States proves his abilities. His diverse background includes: recognized New York actor and comedian, business entrepreneur, president of an advertising agency, and he has even designed rockets.

Dr. Powell is the author of numerous books and publications including the best-seller, *Money and You, Silva Mind Mastery for the '90s, Think Wealth... Put Your Money Where Your Mind Is!, Slash Your Mortgage In Half,* and *Taming the Wild Pendulum.* His books have been translated into seventeen languages.

When he is not expanding the minds of people around the globe, Dr. Powell spends his time in St. Petersburg, Florida, were his wife and partner, Dr. Judith Powell, another well-established lecturer, author and self-improvement counselor, live with their three Scottish Terriers, Master, Buddha and Isis.

CAROL HOWELL MILLS

Carol Howell Mills was born in Norfolk, Virginia, where, as a young child, she played within walking distance of the Edgar Cayce Institute. All of her life she has had first-hand experience being the "different" child, or the "misfit." She has truly lived the world of a "psychic child."

Ms. Mills received her Bachelors degree from Valdosta State College, Georgia, her Masters from the University of Tampa, Florida, and is presently working on her Educational Specialist degree. She has received a Masters Certification in metaphysical studies, and has been awarded an Honorary Dame Doctorate degree for her contribution to mankind. Her studies continue in the fields of education and metaphysics, having studied under several well-known teachers.

Carol is a dedicated person; a well-rounded and committed educator in the Hillsborough County school system in Florida. In the past several years, she has become director of her own individualized instructional school for children of all ages, which fosters the idea that everyone is gifted and has the potential to discover their talents — given time, understanding, patience and a willingness to discover it.

Ms. Mills resides in Tampa, Florida, where she enjoys her collections of Mount St. Helen glass, Charles Dickens' village, and her 250 teddy bears. Carol makes use of her enjoyment of traveling cross-country as an opportunity to add to her collections. She shares her home with her cockatiel, Squeekie Jackson.

GLOSSARY

Astral Body: a body composed of fine matter, extending beyond the denser physical body. It does not feel pain or outer sensations; it conveys emotions and desires to the physical body.

Astral Travel: when the astral body separates from the physical body, as during sleep, or under the influence of drugs or as the result of accidents — and travels in the Astral Plane (the world of emotions, desires and passions).

Aura: a luminous radiation energy (vital force) surrounding a given body (usually the head) or object, that is said to take on different colors, indicative of the kind of thought and character of the person. The halo. Physical, astral and spiritual energies blended and occuping the same space.

Clairaudience: the faculty of "hearing" with the mental "inner" ear. Extrasensory perception of messages; hearing sounds or voices of people living in the past, present and in the future.

Clairaudient: term given to a person who hears voices from within their own minds.

Clairsensience: the faculty of feeling or sensing (smelling) the tactile or emotional aspects of people, places and things, who or which are not objectively present in the environment.

Clairsensient: term given to a person who empathetically feels (smells) the physical or emotional highs and lows of people, animals, plants and objects.

Clairvoyance: the faculty of perceiving objects or events, without having previous knowledge about those objects or events. "Seeing" with the mind's eye.

Clairvoyant: term given to a person who displays clairvoyance.

Color: modulation of energy.

Consciousness: the intelligent focusing of awareness.

Dreams: a series of thoughts, images and emotions taking an inner-vision format during sleep. Dreams occur during REM (Rapid Eye Movement).

Daydream: an enjoyable visual creation of the imagination.

ESP Cards: used by J. B. Rhine, contains 25 cards, each bearing one of the following five symbols: star, circle, square, cross and waves (three parallel wavy lines).

ESP: generally stands for Extra Sensory Perception or psychic (PSI) abilities. Overall general term for psychic abilities — the experience of or response to a specific object, mental or spiritual state, event or outside physical influence without the actual sensory input or contact. *The definition we prefer is Effective Sensory Projection.*

Healing, Laying-on of Hands: the direction, modulation and exchange of energies from one person's hands (the healer) to the body of the subject, plant or animal.

Inner-Conscious: awareness through the sixth-sense (psychic sense).

Meditator: a term given to a person who meditates; who alters their consciousness from the outer world to the inner world of mind and soul.

Meditation: mental relaxation techniques to alter the brainwave frequencies from Beta (14-20 cycles per second) to Alpha (7-14 cps) and to Theta (5-14 cps).

Mental Projection: to extend or project one's thought-picture to another place or time, to another person or into an object or animal.

Mind: the element(s) in a living being that feels, perceives, thinks, wills and reasons through conscious thought.

Outer-Conscious: awareness through your five senses.

Parapsychology: a branch of science that deals with PSI communication, i.e. behavioral or personal exchanges which are extra sensorimotor — not dependent on the senses nor muscles.

Past Lives: previous incarnations apparently embodied by the same soul. Past life information may be obtained through Age Regression and hypnotic trance states.

Precognition: prediction of future events, i.e. random events, the occurrence of which cannot be inferred from present knowledge.

PSI: see ESP.

PSI-hit: when the subject correctly guesses, is right on target for that which they are attempting.

Psychic: a term given to a person sensitive to non-physical forces and influences.

Psychic Abilities (PSI): developed "gifts" of prophesy, psychokinesis and telepathy.

Psychokinesis (PK): The ability to move things with your mind power only, with no outside influences.

Psychometry: term used to denote the faculty of "reading," the characteristics of people (places or things) by holding in the hand small objects, i.e. a watch or ring, which a person has had in their possession.

Prophesy: same as precognition.

Prophet: a term given to a person who displays abilities to see into the future; to predict events that *may* occur in the future.

Reincarnation: rebirth in new bodies or forms of life; i.e. the rebirth of a soul into a human body (for apparent new lessons to be learned).

Sender: the person who projects with their mind mental images to the "receiver" without any physical contact.

Soul: spiritual essence of every individual human being. It is immortal.

Subject: the "Receiver" in tests, games or other psychic experiments, of the mental images being sent by the "sender." Also the person whose ESP abilities are being tested in an experiment (or game).

Telekinesis: the production of motion in objects without contact or other physical means.

Telepathic: term given to a person who displays telepathic powers.

Telepathy: mind-to-mind communication through extrasensory means. *Thought transference.*

BIBLIOGRAPHY AND SUGGESTED READINGS

Addington, Jack and Cornelia, *Drawing the Larger Circle: How to Love and be Loved.* DeVorss and Co., California, 1985.

Binder, Betty B., *Past Life Regression Guidebook.* Reincarnation Books/Tapes, California, 1991.

Bristol, Claude M., *The Magic of Believing.* Pocket Books, New York, 1969.

Cayce, Edgar, "Advise to Parents" Circulating File#450001, Edgar Cayce Foundation, Virginia, 1971, pp. 1 - 14.

Cayce, Edgar and Hugh Lynn Cayce, "God's Other Door." Association for Research and Enlightenment, Virginia.

Ellis, Ph.D., Albert with Sandra Mosley, and Janet L. Wolfe, *How to Raise an Emotionally Healthy, Happy Child.* Wilshire Book Co., California, 1966.

Fillmore, Charles, *The Revealing Word.* Unity Village, Unity School of Christianity, Missouri, 5th printing, 1979.

Fisher, Joe, *The Case for Reincarnation.* Bantam Books, New York, 1984.

Geller, Uri, *My Story.* Praeger Publishers, New York, 1975.

Hammel, Jeff and Dr. Tag Powell, *How to Start and Run a Psychic Group.* Universal Life and Science Foundation, Florida, 1983.

Krieger, Dolores, Ph.D., RN, *The Therapeutic Touch.* Prentice-Hall, Inc., New Jersey, 1979.

Leshan, Lawrence, *How to Meditate: A Guide to Self Discovery.* Little Brown, Massachusetts, 1974.

Ouseley, S.G.J., *Colour Meditations.* L.N. Fowler and Company Ltd., 11th printing, England, 1974.

Powell, Dr. Tag and Dr. Judith, *Silva Mind Mastery for the 90's.* Top of the Mountain Publishing, Florida, 1991.

Retallack, Dorothy, *Sound of Music and Plants.* DeVorss & Co., California, 1978.

Rhine, Louisa E., *PSI, What Is It?* Harper & Row, Publishers, Inc., New York, 1975.

Silva, Jose & Philip Miele. *The Silva Mind Control Method.* Simon & Schuster Pocket Books, New York, 1978.

Silva, Laura, *For Parents Only: The Silva Mind Control Method,* Institute of Psychorientology, Inc., Texas, 1982.

Stone, Robert B. Ph.D., *The Secret Life of Your Cells.* Whitford Press, Pennsylvania, 1989.

Strauss, Sally, *Inner Rhythm.* Chase Publication, California, 1985.

Sutphen, Dick, *Past Lives, Future Lives.* Pocket Books, New York, 1982.

Sutphen, Dick, *You Were Born to be Together.* Pocket Books, New York, 1982.

Tompkins, Peter and Christopher Bird, *The Secret Life of Plants.* Harper & Row Publishers, Inc., New York, 1973.

Vaughan, Alan, "Learning to be Intuitive," *Venture Inward,* Nov./Dec. 1992, Association for Research and Enlightenment, Virginia, pp. 18 - 20.

Wambach, Helen Ph.D., *Reliving Past Lives, The Evidence Under Hypnosis.* Harper & Row Publishers, Inc., New York, 1978.

Weed, Joseph J., *Psychic Energy: How to Change Desires into Realities.* Parker Publishing Company, Inc., New York, 1970.

Weiss, Brian L., M.D., *Many Lives, Many Masters.* Simon & Schuster, Inc., New York, 1988.

Wyatt, Valerie, *Amazing Investigations.* Prentice-Hall Books For Young Readers, New York, 1987.

Index

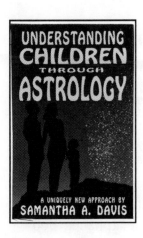

UNDERSTANDING CHILDREN THROUGH ASTROLOGY

by Samantha A. Davis

This bold new concept gives you secret insights for building successful relationships with your children. You will learn the *five facets of the astrological personality*, and how they are expressed differently in each individual... accentuating their strengths and building upon their astrological weaknesses.

A great book for the parent, guardian, therapist, counselor and teacher! This new approach will save everyone time, energy and frustration when communicating with children. At the reader's fingertips is *a complete reference of guides*... references for every sign, for every child... covering the two luminaries — Sun, Moon; and the three personal planets — Mercury, Mars and Venus. A uniquely new approach to using Astrology as a method for determining the individuality of each child... and the Inner Child within you!

ISBN 1-56087-050-8, 304 pages, US$14.95 + $3.00sh

SILVA MIND MASTERY FOR THE '90s

by Dr. Tag Powell and Dr. Judith Powell

The how-to best-seller using the very latest research combined with the world's largest mind development training. Already translated into seventeen languages, the demand continues because of its practical applications and tools to easily improve your business and personal life. *Mind Mastery* covers: how to visualize, instant attitude adjustment, leadership skills, and creativity. Special techniques to improve relationships, sales, confidence, memory, and health. *Silva Mind Mastery for the '90s* will continue to empower you for years!

ISBN 0-914295-99-3, 256 pages, US$12.95 + $3.00s/h

TOP OF THE MOUNTAIN PUBLISHING
11701 S. Belcher Road, Suite #123
Largo, Florida 34643-5117 U.S.A.
FAX: (813) 536-3681
PHONE: (813) 530-0110

For a FREE Catalog, write, phone or fax:

TOP OF THE MOUNTAIN PUBLISHING

TEL (813) 550-0110